PROPERTY OF NICE COMMUNITY SCHOOLS

Date Out	Name In Ink	Gr.	Condition E. G. F. P.	Fine
	①			

Books are furnished free by the school but damage beyond normal wear and tear must be paid for by the borrower.
NEVER PUT PENCILS OR THICK PAPER IN A BOOK

Rolling Along

CHARLES C. WALCUTT
GLENN McCRACKEN

Consultants:
LEILANI CAMARA
MARGARET R. EMERY
RICHARD C. HUNTER

Lippincott Basic Reading E

HARPER & ROW, Publishers New York   Philadelphia   Hagerstown   San Francisco   London

Acknowledgments

Grateful acknowledgment is made to the following authors and publishers to use copyright materials. Every effort has been made to obtain permission to use previously published material. Any errors or omissions are unintentional and the publisher will be grateful to learn of them.

"My Favorite Word" reprinted from OODLES OF NOODLES, copyright © 1964, by Lucia and James L. Hymes, Jr., a Young Scott Book, by permission of Addison-Wesley Publishing Company, Inc.

"We Could Be Friends" from THE WAY THINGS ARE AND OTHER POEMS by Myra Cohn Livingston (A Margaret K. McElderry Book). Copyright © 1974 by Myra Cohn Livingston. Used by permission of Atheneum Publishers.

"The Library" by Barbara A. Huff from FAVORITE POEMS OLD AND NEW, edited by H. Ferris. Copyright © 1957. Doubleday and Co., Inc. Reprinted by permission of Barbara A. Huff.

Eight Riddles from I KNOW! A RIDDLE BOOK by Jane Sarnoff. Text copyright © 1976 by Jane Sarnoff. Reprinted by permission of Charles Scribner's Sons, Publishers.

"The Turtle Who Wanted to Fly" adapted from "The Turtle Who Wanted to Fly" in PLAYS FROM AFRICAN FOLKTALES by Carol Korty. Copyright © 1969, 1975. By permission of Charles Scribner's Sons, Publishers.

"The Monstrous Glisson Glop" adapted from THE MONSTROUS GLISSON GLOP by Diane Redfield Massie. Text copyright © 1970 by Diane Redfield Massie. By permission of Four Winds Press, a division of Scholastic Magazines, Inc.

"The Terrible Thing That Happened at Our House" adapted from THE TERRIBLE THING THAT HAPPENED AT OUR HOUSE by Marge Blaine. Text copyright © 1975 by Marge Blaine. By permission of Four Winds Press, a division of Scholastic Magazines, Inc.

"The Goat in the Rug" adapted from THE GOAT IN THE RUG by Charles L. Blood and Martin Link. Text copyright © 1976 by Charles L. Blood and Martin Link. Reprinted by permission of Four Winds Press, a division of Scholastic Magazines, Inc.

"Becky and the Bear" adapted by permission of G. P. Putnam's Sons from BECKY AND THE BEAR by Dorothy Van Woerkom. Copyright © 1975 by Dorothy Van Woerkom.

"Story Time" adapted from "Story Time" by Laurence M. Janifer in JOURNEY TO ANOTHER STAR AND OTHER STORIES. Copyright © 1974. Reprinted by permission of Lerner Publications Company, 241 First Avenue North, Minneapolis, Minnesota 55401.

"Eletelephony" from TIRRA LIRRA by Laura Richards. Copyright © 1935 by Laura E. Richards. Copyright © 1960 by Hamilton Richards. By permission of Little, Brown and Company.

"Every Time I Climb a Tree" from ONE AT A TIME by David McCord. Copyright © 1952 by David McCord. By permission of Little, Brown and Company.

(continued on page 249)

Copyright © 1981, 1975 by J. B. Lippincott Company

All rights reserved. No part of this publication may be reproduced in any form or by any means, photographic, electrostatic, or mechanical, or by any information storage and retrieval system or other method, for any use, without written permission from the publisher. Printed in the United States of America
ISBN 0-397-44047-2

Contents

Lisa and the Grompet	1
We Could Be Friends	13
Fire-Safety Tips	14
Monstrous Glisson Glop	22
April Rain Song	33
Clouds Tell About the Weather	34
Riddles	46
Benjamin Franklin—A Great Man	48
Pretend to Be a Printer	59
My Favorite Word	64
Becky and the Bear	65
How Many Neighbors in *Your* Neighborhood?	79
Night Ride	80
Did You Know?	92
School Under the Trees	94
The Library	105
Guy the Bookworm	107
Books on Wheels	116

She'll Be Comin' 'Round the Mountain	122
The Hole in the Dike	128
The Turtle Who Wanted to Fly	137
It's a Small World	157
The Chef's Party	159
Eletelephony	165
The Muffin Muncher	167
The Terrible Thing That Happened at Our House	180
Jonathan George	192
The Goat in the Rug	200
Every Time I Climb a Tree	211
Story Time	213
Rumpelstiltskin	224
Glossary	239

Developmental pages: silent b, silent l—page 12; silent g, silent h, silent gh—page 21; /e/ea, /ā/ea—page 32; /er/ear, /air/ear, /ar/ear—page 45; /ē/ie, /ē/ei— page 63; /ā/ei, /ā/eigh, /ā/ey—page 78; ough—pages 90, 91; /i/y, /ī/uy, /ī/ui, /i/ui— page 104; ai, ue, ile—page 120; silent t, silent n—page 121.

Lisa and the Grompet

Once upon a time, about a week, or maybe a year ago, a little girl named Lisa got tired of being told what to do.

Lisa woke up that morning and her big sister said: "Don't make so much noise. Don't shut the window. Don't bang the shade. Don't knock over the goldfish bowl."

Lisa went downstairs. Her mother said: "Take off that old shirt. And pull up your socks. And don't forget you have a piano lesson today."

And her father said: "Don't step in the dog's dish. And pull up your socks."

"Sit down and eat," said her mother.

Lisa sat down to eat her cereal, toast, and juice.

"Take your vitamin pill and don't spill the milk," said her mother.

Lisa grew crosser and crosser. She gave her vitamin pill to the dog. The dog spit it out.

"I'm tired of being told what to do," said Lisa, and she went outside.

"Every day everybody tells me what to do. I don't like it. I will go away all by myself. I will tell my own self what to do."

And she did. She went along a path near the woods. Lisa looked at the flowers in bloom.

"Nobody says to the flowers, 'Don't forget to bloom tomorrow. Don't forget to wiggle your roots and grow a new leaf because a bug ate one yesterday.'"

Lisa looked at the butterflies flying around her.

"Nobody says to the butterflies, 'Don't sit on that flower! Sit on this one!'"

Lisa looked back down the path. She didn't see her house anymore.

"There," said Lisa. "I have run away."

She sat down to rest and think about things.

Lisa noticed a funny noise. She looked all around. She did not see anything.

Then something pinched her.

"Ow!" said Lisa.

She looked down. Something very small was making a popping sound and jumping up and down.

"What are you?" asked Lisa.

"*A grompet. A grompet. A grompet!*" yelled the grompet. "You sat on my front yard and squashed it."

"I'm sorry," said Lisa. "I didn't know it was your front yard."

"Well it was," said the grompet. "And you squashed it. Don't forget to LOOK before you sit down!"

Lisa looked at the grompet. "You sound like my mother."

The grompet came up close and looked at Lisa. Lisa looked at the grompet.

"NOW what did I do?" asked Lisa. "I told you I was sorry I squashed your front yard."

"When you wreck somebody's front yard," said the grompet, "the least you can do is ask them to tell you the story of their life."

"I'm sorry," said Lisa. "I didn't know I was supposed to ask the story of your life."

"You sound like my Uncle George!" shouted the grompet. And he burst into tears.

"Poor Grompet," said Lisa. "I know how you feel. I am running away because I am always being told what to do. It makes me mad and sad, and everything smashes and spills, and everybody yells."

The grompet stopped crying. "Don't tell me the story of YOUR life," he yelled.

"I'm sorry," said Lisa.

"OK then," said the grompet. "I'll tell you mine. My Uncle George never told me to eat my cereal or pull up my socks or take my vitamin pill. He didn't tell me to do anything. So I just stood there and shrank.

I was afraid I was going to shrink into Nothing At All, so I ran away. Nobody told me to go home, so I never did. All I know is I am a grompet and I am very small and very sad."

They both sat thinking. Then Lisa said, "Everybody tells me what to do and it's just awful."

The grompet came closer. He looked at Lisa, and Lisa looked at him.

"If you like, you can tell me what to do," whispered the grompet.

"What a wonderful idea!" Lisa jumped up and . . .

"NOW look what you've done!" shouted the grompet. He had tumbled over onto his stomach, and was stuck under a mushroom.

Lisa started to help the grompet up, but she changed her mind.

"Don't be silly!" she scolded. "Get out from under that mushroom this minute. And don't forget to brush yourself off."

The grompet stopped looking angry and began to smile.

He crawled out from under the mushroom and brushed himself off.

He came over to Lisa. Lisa picked him up and set him on her knee. She picked a leaf out of his beard for him.

The grompet smiled.

Lisa smiled, too.

"I love you," said the grompet.

"And I love you," said Lisa. "I'll take you home with me and take care of you. I'll even take you to school. And I'll tell you what to do all the time."

"And I'll be happy," said the grompet. "I'll never ever shrink into Nothing At All!"

"We are going home for lunch now," said Lisa. "After lunch we have a piano lesson. Don't forget."

They got home just as Lisa's mother was saying, "Lisa! Wash your hands and face. Lunch is ready. Hurry up!"

"Yes, Mother," said Lisa.

She went upstairs and put the grompet beside the washbowl.

"Wash your wings and face, Grompet," she said. "And don't forget behind your ears."

The grompet washed his wings and face and behind his ears, and Lisa helped dry him off.

Lisa and the grompet had soup, peanut butter sandwiches, and fruit for lunch.

"Don't get your beard in the soup or the soup in your beard, Grompet," said Lisa.

The grompet was so happy he ate all his lunch. Lisa was so happy she ate all her lunch. And she didn't spill a thing.

After lunch Lisa and the grompet sat down at the piano.

"Be very still, Grompet," said Lisa, "while I practice."

The grompet smiled. "I love you," he said.

"I love you," said Lisa, and she began to play.

silent b

comb	bomb	limb	climb
dumb	numb	thumb	crumb
plumber	lamb	debt	doubt

silent l

talk	talking	walk	walking
sidewalk	stalk	chalk	folks
calm	palm	balmy	half
calf	should	would	could

We Could Be Friends

We could be friends
Like friends are supposed to be.
You, picking up the telephone
Calling me
    to come over and play
    or take a walk,
    finding a place
    to sit and talk,
Or just goof around
Like friends do,
Me, picking up the telephone
Calling you.

Myra Cohn Livingston

Fire-Safety Tips

Before Benjamin Franklin discovered electricity, people had to cook food over a wood or coal fire. They used fire to keep warm, and sometimes to see by.

There is no doubt that the first person who made a fire discovered something wonderful. Fire is very useful. But fire can also be very dangerous. Each year, thousands of people are burned or killed in fires. Sometimes these fires could have been prevented.

Each year valuable property is lost by fire. Forests, homes, and stores are burned to the ground.

Most fires seem to be caused by carelessness. Many fires are started by children playing with matches. Fires are also started by people being careless when smoking or when using portable heaters. Many fires start in the kitchen. When cooking at the stove or using an electric appliance, you should stay close by.

The very best way to stop a fire is to prevent it from starting in the first place. Every home should have at least one smoke detector. A smoke detector makes a loud buzzing sound when smoke hits it. This sound warns you that a fire could be starting somewhere in the house. Many fires start when people are sleeping. The smoke alarm can wake you up and give you more time to get out safely.

The following safety tips can save lives. They are important to remember:

1. PLAN A HOME FIRE DRILL. Talk with your folks and decide on the two best ways to get out quickly. Decide how to get out of rooms on the second or third floors. If a rope or ladder is needed, keep it near a window. Practice your home fire drill as if a fire had really started.

2. SLEEP WITH BEDROOM DOORS CLOSED. This should help to keep out heat and smoke if a fire starts while you are sleeping.

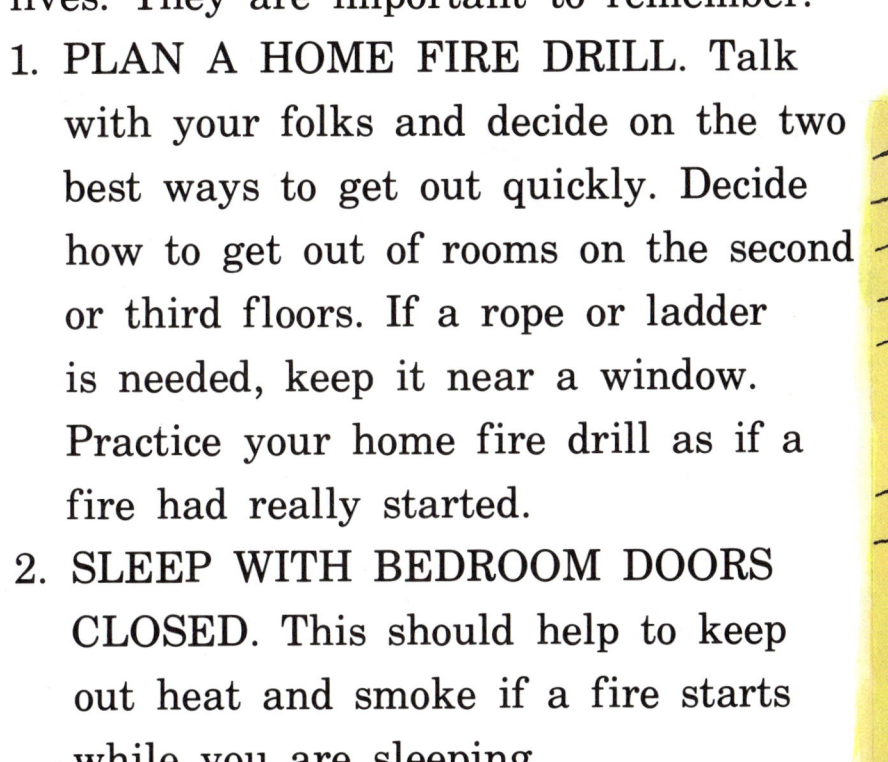

3. **STAY CALM.** Fire is scary, but try not to panic. Yell, "FIRE!" and pound on the wall to wake up or warn others.

4. **FEEL ANY DOOR BEFORE YOU OPEN IT.** Put the palm of your hand on the door. If the door is cool, open it just a crack. Close the door quickly if heat or smoke rushes in. If the door feels hot, do not open it.

5. GO TO A WINDOW. If you can't open it, smash the glass with a chair or some large object. Watch out for flying glass as you smash the window. Shout for help. Do not try to jump by yourself. Stay at the window until help comes.

6. STAY CLOSE TO THE FLOOR. Remember that heat and smoke rise. If there is smoke in the room, you will be able to breathe best if you are close to the floor. When it is safe to get out of the room, crawl to the nearest exit.

7. IF YOUR CLOTHES CATCH ON FIRE, DON'T RUN. Roll on the ground to smother the fire. You could also put the fire out by wrapping a blanket, small rug, or a coat around you.

Following these fire-safety tips may save your life, your family, and friends. But remember, the best thing for everyone is to practice fire prevention every day.

BE ALERT. HELP PREVENT FIRES.

PLAN and PRACTICE NOW!

silent g

| gnat | gnaw | gnome | sign |

silent h

| oh | hour | honor | honest |
| herb | ghost | exhaust | exhibit |

silent gh

right	night	might	sight
light	fight	flight	fright
bright	sigh	high	thigh
straight	caught	taught	daughter

The Monstrous Glisson Glop

There was a monstrous Glisson Glop
Who lived beneath the sea.
His eyes were red. His teeth were sharp
And greener than a pea.

"I love to dine on lantern fish,
And eels are better yet.
The more I eat," the monster said,
"The darker, still, it gets!"

"It's gloomy on the ocean floor.
It's blacker than the night.
And if I eat the lantern fish,
There won't be any light."

He ate another lantern fish
And swallowed down an eel.
"A pity!" said the Glisson Glop.
"How sad it makes me feel."

He found his tattered storybook
And held it to his face.
"I can't make out the words," he said.
"I'll never find my place!"

"I mustn't eat another eel!"
An eel came swimming by.
He gulped it up and licked his chops.
"It makes me want to cry!"

"The sea is black as ink," he said.
"It's hard to see my claws.
If lantern fish come swimming by,
I'm buttoning my jaws."

The lantern fish came swimming past.
He ate them one by one.
"I've finished off the lantern fish,
And now," he sighed, "there's none."

"What *will* I do?" He wrung his claws.
"A Glisson Glop needs light!
I'm frightened of the dark!" he said.
"Somehow this isn't right!"

A little fish came swimming by
With lights above his head.
The Glisson Glop fell on his knees.
"A LIGHT!" the monster said.

"Stay here!" he told the little fish.
"Come near so I can see!"
"Why should I?" said the little fish.
"Perhaps you might eat *me*."

"Perhaps I won't," the Glisson Glop
Said crossly from his bed.
"I hate the dark. It strains my eyes
And makes them very red."

"My promises," the Glisson Glop
Said, "hopefully are good.
I try my best to keep them.
When I don't, I know I should."

"I'm going!" said the little fish.
He quickly swam away.
"Outrageous!" said the Glisson Glop.
"What *can* a monster say?"

He lay upon the ocean floor.
"It's day . . . or is it night?"
"One can't," he said, "tell what it is.
I wish I had a light."

"I wish I had a lantern fish
And one electric eel.
I'd never think again," he said,
"Of making them a meal."

"I'd treat them very gently.
I'd pat them on the head.
I'd read them bedtime stories, too,
Before they went to bed."

The Glisson Glop sat sadly down
And strained his eyes to see.
"The black is even blacker
Than it ever used to be."

"What's that?" he said. "Some little
 lights!
THEY'RE COMING NEAR! HOORAY!
A lantern fish and eel," he said,
"Are surely on their way!"

A lantern fish swam slowly by
A blue electric eel.
"I PROMISE NOT TO EAT YOU!
OH, HOW WONDERFUL I FEEL!"

The lantern fish and eel swam down.
They climbed upon his knee.
And now the monster reads at night.
"It's hard," he says, "when one can't bite
Or nibble up one's reading light.
But *oh*! It's nice to see."

ea as short e

head	read	dead	lead
bread	thread	dread	ready
spread	deaf	breakfast	health
healthy	wealthy	meant	feather
leather	weather	heavy	sweat
breath	meadow	pleasant	instead

ea as long a

great	steak	break	daybreak

April Rain Song

Let the rain kiss you.
Let the rain beat upon your head
   with silver liquid drops.
Let the rain sing you a lullaby.
The rain makes still pools
   on the sidewalk.
The rain makes running pools
   in the gutter.
The rain plays a little sleep-song
   on our roof at night.
And I love the rain.

Langston Hughes

Clouds Tell About the Weather

People have always wanted to know about the weather. Long ago, farmers began to watch clouds in the sky. They knew that clouds meant drops of water were collecting. *Is a storm headed this way?* they wondered. *Will we get the rain we need?*

Sailors watched the clouds, too. At daybreak they asked themselves, *Will we get a strong wind to fill our sails? How far can we travel today?*

At breakfast time children looked out their windows. On cold mornings they wondered, *Will it snow today?* On summer days they looked at the sky and asked themselves, *Will this be a great day for a picnic?*

All of these people knew that different kinds of clouds would bring different kinds of weather. Which clouds meant good weather? Which clouds meant bad?

Some clouds are low in the sky. They are dark and heavy looking. These clouds often drop rain on us. Other clouds are very high in the sky. They look light and fluffy. These clouds never bring rain.

Clouds form in different shapes and sizes. Each kind of cloud has a name. People have discovered that when the clouds change, the weather changes, too.

What do you see in these clouds? Do you see great big feathers? Do you see curls of hair? These are called *cirrus* clouds. *Cirrus* is the Latin word for hair. Cirrus clouds float across the top of the sky. They are thin and look very light. They mean pleasant weather.

These clouds are called *cumulus* clouds. *Cumulus* is a Latin word that means heap. Some people think cumulus clouds look like heaps of whipped cream. Other people see fat sheep or puffy loaves of bread. What do you see when you look at these clouds?

Little cumulus clouds mean pleasant weather. But sometimes these little clouds grow. They get big and heavy. They move lower in the sky. The little sheep turn into great big elephants. Watch out! The weather is changing.

Sometimes the cumulus clouds keep growing. They begin to look like dark mountains with flat tops. Then they are

called *thunderheads*. Thunderheads can bring dreadful weather!

Sometimes the wind breaks up the thunderheads. The dark mountains turn back into little sheep, and the sun shines again. But if no wind stops the thunderheads, it is time to get ready to head for home. Heavy rain, lightning, and thunder are on the way.

These clouds are called *stratus* clouds. *Stratus* comes from a Latin word that means spread out. These clouds spread out across the sky. Sometimes stratus clouds look like a thin white sheet. They mean good weather.

Sometimes stratus clouds come close to the ground. This is what causes fog.

People are always trying to find out more about the weather. Today we use airplanes, balloons, and even satellites in space to take pictures of the clouds. These pictures tell us how the clouds are moving and changing all over our planet. This information is used to help

us write weather reports. Most of the time, the reports that are read on radio and TV are right. But sometimes the weather surprises us.

No one can ever really be sure when the clouds will change. The only thing we can be sure of is that nothing changes more than the weather.

ear as er

earn	early	earth	search
learn	learning	heard	pearl

ear as air

bear	pear	wear	tear

ear as ar

heart   hearth

Riddles

1. Why can't ducks fly upside down?
   They will quack up.

2. What did the flower say to the bee?
   Can I be your honey?

3. What do you get when you cross an insect with a rabbit?
   Bugs Bunny.

4. Which runs faster, hot or cold?
   Hot. Everybody can catch cold.

5. What did the monster eat after its teeth were pulled?
   The dentist.

6. What is still dirty when a dirty kid has finished taking a bath?
   The bathtub.

7. What has two hands, but no feet?
   A clock.

8. What holiday do all the vampires like best?
   Fangsgiving.

Benjamin Franklin—
A Great Man

It was the summer of 1716 in Boston, Massachusetts. Mill Pond was crowded with children. It was the best place to swim in the whole city. One day everyone stopped swimming to watch something unusual.

"Look at Ben go!" one boy cried. "Benjamin Franklin, how can you swim so fast?"

Ten-year-old Ben Franklin soon shared his secret. He had tied wooden paddles to his hands and feet. "These paddles help me go fast," he replied.

"Did you learn this from a book?" Ben's brother asked. Ben's brother knew that Ben loved to read books which told him how to do things.

"No," said Ben. "It was my own idea. One day I saw bears swimming in Boston Bay. I noticed that bears have big paddle-shaped paws. That's why they can swim fast. So I made these wooden paddles for myself. I can swim fast, but not very far. The paddles are too heavy."

Then Ben smiled. He was getting another idea. The next day Ben went for a swim holding onto a kite string. The kite flew over Mill Pond. While Ben held the string, the kite pulled him quickly all the way across the pond.

Ben liked to learn from other people and from books. But most of all, he liked trying out his own ideas. He was always searching for new ways to do things better.

Ben's family was very large. His parents had seventeen children. Ben was one of the youngest in the family. He was the only one to go to school. At the time Ben lived, very few children went to school. Most children learned by helping their parents at home and at work. Ben went to school for three years. When he was ten years old, he went to work for his father. Ben helped him make candles and soap.

Ben worked hard. But he knew in his heart that making candles was not what he wanted to do. So when he was twelve years old, Ben went to live with his brother James. He was a printer and owned his own newspaper. Ben learned all about printing from James.

Finally Ben felt he was ready to earn his own living. When he was seventeen he decided to go to Philadelphia. There he worked as a printer during the day. At night he wrote and read books.

Ben saved most of the money he earned. Soon he was able to open his own printing shop. He even started his own newspaper and called it the *Pennsylvania Gazette*. People liked Ben's newspaper. It was full of new ideas, just like Ben.

Benjamin Franklin was the first person in America to use pictures in a newspaper. His newspaper looked better than the others, too. He used darker ink and whiter paper.

In Ben's time almost everyone in America looked forward to getting a new almanac each year. Almanacs printed weather forecasts, advice, news, and important dates for farmers and sailors.

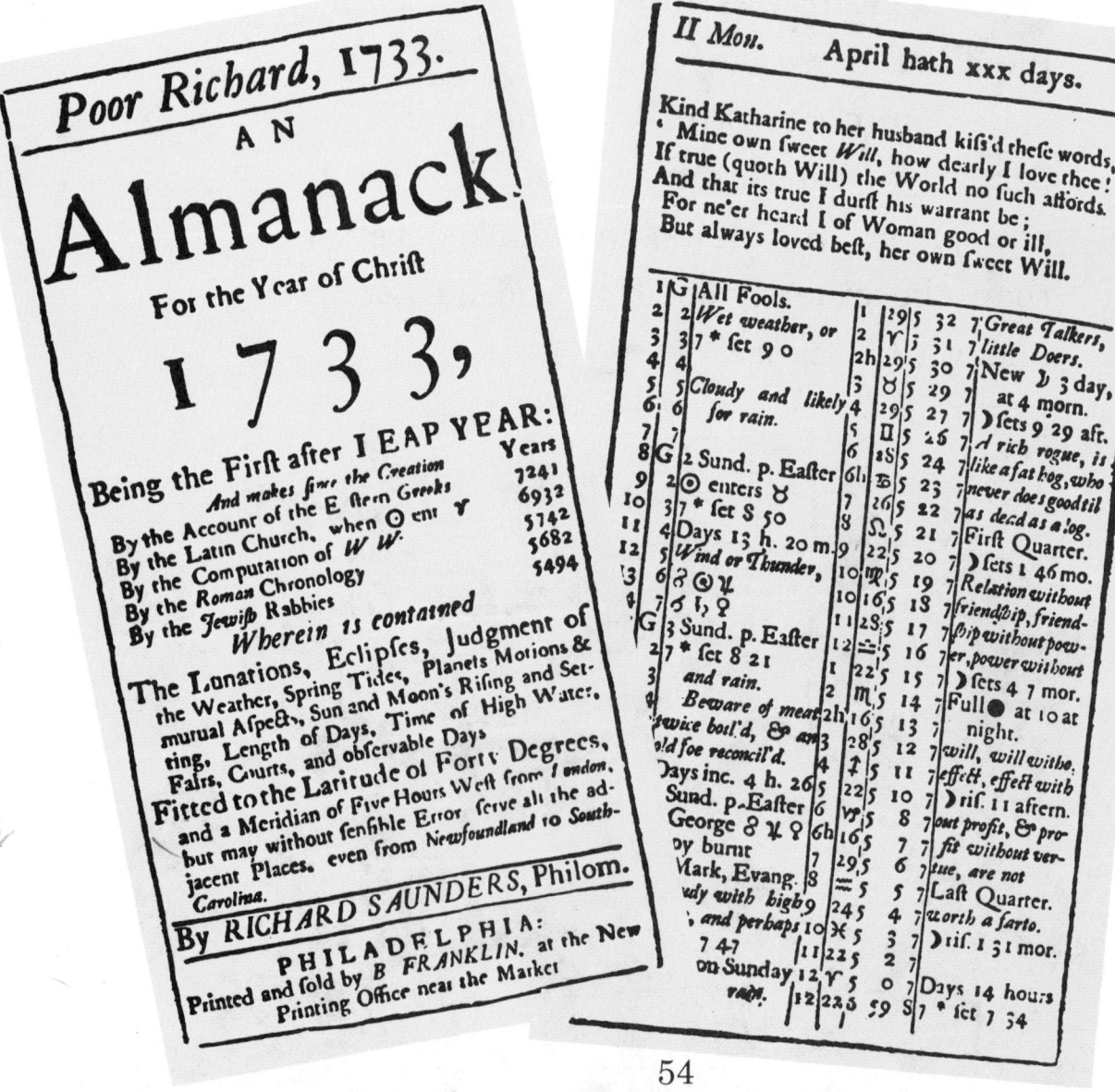

When Ben was twenty-six, he had an idea for a new kind of almanac. His book had facts, but it also had jokes and clever sayings. Ben called the book *Poor Richard's Almanac.*

Ben made up the character of Poor Richard and made up all the things he said. People liked to read about the funny things Poor Richard did. They also liked his wise sayings. Ben's almanac became famous.

Here are some of Poor Richard's sayings that can still be heard today:

"Early to bed, and early to rise makes a man healthy, wealthy, and wise."

"A penny saved is a penny earned."

"A small leak can sink a great ship."

When Benjamin Franklin wasn't printing newspapers or writing almanacs, he was thinking of ways to improve Philadelphia. Ben came up with ideas for a public library, a fire department, and a hospital.

He also suggested cleaning the streets, putting up street lights, and improving the mail service. Philadelphia became a better place to live because of Ben's ideas.

Sometimes Ben's ideas turned into inventions. He invented a stove that could heat a whole house. This is now known as a Franklin stove.

Ben also invented a new kind of eyeglasses called *bifocals*. The bottom half of these glasses helped Ben read; the top half helped him see things that were far away.

Ben had other great ideas that he turned into inventions. One was a chair with a writing table attached to the arm. Another was a chair that could be unfolded into a stepladder.

Ben did experiments to prove his ideas were correct. Then he wrote down all that he saw and heard. In one of his most famous experiments, Ben proved that lightning is electricity.

When the United States of America was formed, Ben was asked to help write the laws and run the government of the new country.

Today we still read Poor Richard's clever sayings. We still use Franklin stoves, bifocals, and many of his other inventions as well. We even live by the laws he helped to write. As you can see, Benjamin Franklin's ideas are as great today as they were in his day.

Pretend to Be a Printer

Early in his life, Ben Franklin learned to be a printer. He learned how to print pictures as well as words. Ben liked to make his own picture printers. He used them to print pictures in his newspapers and almanacs. You can use shapes to make your own picture printers.

Shape Picture Printer

To make a shape picture printer you will need:
- a crayon or pencil
- two sheets of cardboard, one sheet a little larger than the other
- scissors
- white glue
- poster paint
- a small paintbrush
- drawing paper

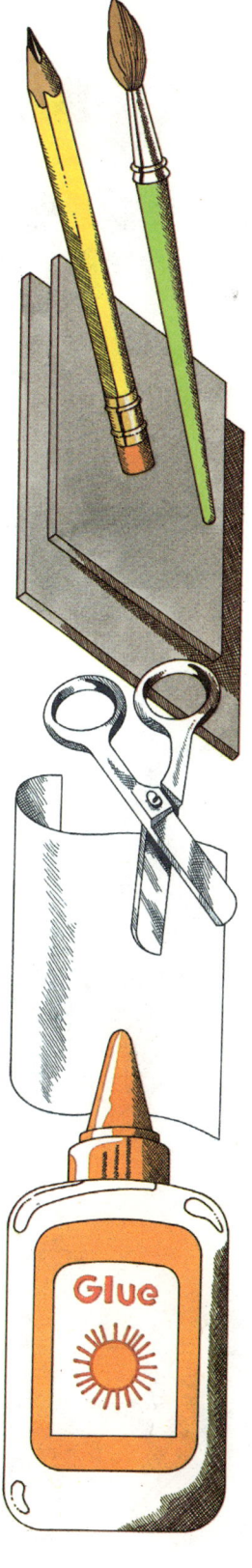

Now, starting with step 1—

1. Draw or trace a shape on one sheet of cardboard. The shape can be a circle ○ , a triangle △ , or a rectangle ▭ . But you may wish to pick a more unusual shape. You can use a heart ♡ , a pear ⬳ , or a teddy bear 🐻 .

2. Cut out your shape. Make the shape a little smaller than the other sheet of cardboard.

3. Glue the shape in the center of the second sheet of cardboard.

4. Have a sheet of drawing paper ready on which to print the shape you made.

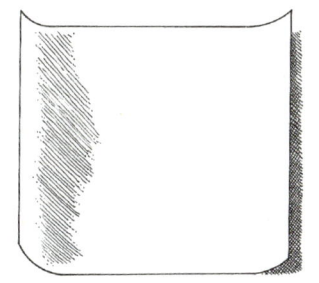 

5. Put a thin coat of paint over the shape only. Do not let the paint dry!

6. Turn the shape printer over. Carefully press it onto the drawing paper.

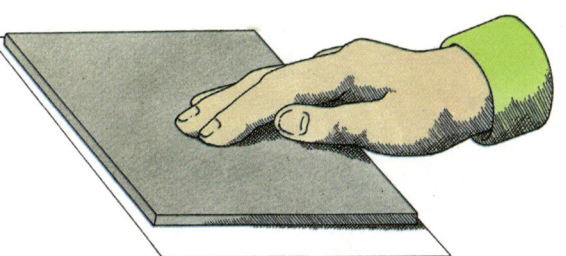

7. Lift the shape printer off the paper. Surprise! There is your shape, printed in color.

8. To make an interesting pattern, print your shape again and again. If the paint dries, put another coat of paint on your shape. You can even mix different shapes and colors.

Save the shape printers you make. Use them when you want to make your own cards, gift wrapping paper, or pictures.

ie as long e

chief	thief	brief	grief
belief	relief	shriek	shield
field	yield	piece	niece
grieve	relieve	believe	achieve
berry	lady	penny	puppy
berries	ladies	pennies	puppies

ei as long e

ceiling receive either neither

My Favorite Word

There is one word—
My favorite—
The very, very best.
It isn't No or Maybe,
It's Yes, Yes, Yes, *Yes*, YES!

"Yes, yes, you may," and
"Yes, of course," and
"Yes, please help yourself."
And when I want a piece of cake,
"Why, yes. It's on the shelf."

Some candy? "Yes."
A cookie? "Yes."
A movie? "Yes, we'll go."

I love it when they say my word:
Yes, *Yes,* YES! (Not No.)

Lucia and James L. Hymes, Jr.

Becky and the Bear

"We will be home before dark," Father said. He stood at the door with his musket.

"Good-bye, Granny," said Ned. "We'll think of you as we eat our corn cakes."

Granny sighed. "We can't eat corn cakes all winter. We must have meat to keep strong and well."

"It has been a hard year," Father said. "With so little rain in the spring, there isn't much food in the forest for the animals. Many of them have gone across the river to live."

"But, Granny," Ned promised, "we'll bring something back today."

Becky watched Father and Ned walk across the field.

"I wish I could go hunting!" she said. Granny laughed. "You're only seven years old," she said.

"Ned could shoot a musket before he was seven," Becky said. "Ned is brave and Father is brave. I want to do something brave, too."

"You don't need to shoot a musket to be brave," Granny told her. "You were brave when your Mama died of the fever. And right now you can stir the hasty pudding."

"Stirring the hasty pudding is not being brave," Becky said, pouting.

Suddenly they heard someone shouting outside.

"Granny! Granny Willow!" It was Paul Benson. Granny and Becky hurried to the door.

"Ma's hurt herself on the wool shears," Paul cried.

Granny took her basket of herbs. "I'll go right back with you," she told Paul. "I hope I won't be long, Becky. But keep the pudding stirred until I get back, and pick some huckleberries for supper."

Becky gave the pudding a stir so it wouldn't stick to the pot. "This is not being brave," Becky said to herself. "And neither is picking huckleberries."

She swung a wooden pail over her arm and crossed the yard to the little shed where the horse and pigs lived. "Next year we'll have pork," Becky said to herself. "But this year the pigs are too young."

Behind the shed were bushes covered with the small berries. Becky picked berries until her pail was nearly full. Then she heard a noise in the bushes. Could it be a thief? She stood still. More noise came from the bushes. Becky saw a huge, fierce-looking black bear! For a brief moment it did not see her. Suddenly the bear lifted its head. It sniffed the air. The bear smelled Becky! She turned and ran back toward the house. Behind her, the bear growled.

She could hear the bushes snap as it came after her. Becky reached the doorstep and looked back. The bear was right behind her! It stood up on its hind legs and struck at her with its paw.

"No!" she shrieked. She ran into the house and slammed the door. The bear growled and snarled. "Maybe it will get tired and go away," Becky said to herself. "But what if it goes into the shed and kills the pigs?"

There was a gun over the fireplace, but she didn't know how to use it. Now the bear was trying to dig a hole under the door. Becky was worried. She knew she had to do something right away. "Maybe I can give him something to

eat," she said to herself. "I believe bears like sweet things."

There was a pot of molasses on the table. And Becky knew where Father kept the rum.

"I'll make a *flip* for the bear!" she cried. She mixed up the ingredients as fast as she could and poured the flip into a bowl.

She carried it to the window and slowly pushed one of the shutters open.

Her hand was shaking. She almost spilled the flip. Gently, she put the bowl on the windowsill. Then she closed the shutter, BANG.

The bear heard the noise. It came to the window. She watched it between the cracks in the shutter. It stood on its hind legs and sniffed. It found the dish. The bear made a funny noise as it drank. Then the bear was gone.

Becky waited at the window for a long, long time. It was very quiet.

At last she went outside. She found the bear near the shed . . . asleep. The flip had worked! The bear was still asleep when Granny came home.

"Well!" said Granny. "Mrs. Benson has a sore hand, but I believe my herbs will soon mend it." She looked at Becky.

"Why do you look so worried, child?" she asked.

"Oh, Granny!" Becky cried. "Come and see what happened!"

Becky and Granny looked down at the sleeping bear.

"Get me a rope from the shed," said Granny. "And don't make a sound."

Becky scurried out to the shed and found a piece of rope. Granny and Becky tied the rope around the stump of a tree. Granny made a noose at the other end of the rope. She slipped it over the bear's head. Now the bear would surely wake up. But the bear slept on.

"There!" Granny said with relief.

"Now I wonder why that bear isn't waking up?"

"It's because I gave him a bowl of flip," said Becky. "I made it with molasses and rum! Remember last year at the Benson's party how their hog got into the flip and drank it all? It ran around the field and fell right down asleep. Father said the rum made it sleepy."

"Well," Granny said, "you surely used your head. When your father comes home, he will shoot the bear before it hurts anyone. Tomorrow you and I will prepare the meat and boil down the fat."

The sun was just going down when Ned and Father came home. They were dirty. They looked very tired.

"What did you bring?" Granny asked. "What did you catch?"

"Nothing!" said Father. "We hunted all day and caught nothing."

"Well," Granny said, smiling, "Becky caught something today." Granny and Becky took Father and Ned to see the bear. It was still asleep. Becky told them how she caught the bear with flip.

Father laughed. "We'll have some good meals and a warm rug," he said, "thanks to our clever Becky."

"And lots of good fat to burn in our lamps," said Granny.

Father put his hand on Becky's head. "Catching a bear was a brave thing to do," he said. Becky smiled . . . but only for a minute.

"Oh!" she cried. "I forgot all about stirring the pudding!"

ei as long a

veil   vein   reins   reindeer

eigh as long a

eight   eighteen   neigh   neighbor
sleigh   weigh   weight   freight

ey as long a

they   whey   prey   obey

How Many Neighbors in YOUR Neighborhood?

Eight?

Eighteen?

Eighty?

How many neighbors doesn't matter—
It can be eighty, eighteen, or eight.
What matters is the friends you have,
'Cause friends make life just great!

Peg Chagnon

Night Ride

It was a bright, moonlit night and the earth was covered with snow. Heather sat next to the hearth where a warm fire was crackling. She wanted so much to go for a long walk in the snow, but Mom and Dad were both busy.

Then she heard a jingling noise. She ran to the window and looked out. There was a sleigh with silver bells! It was pulled by two black horses, and sitting inside were Heather's neighbors, Mr. and Mrs. Creighton and their son Willie.

"Heather! Come with us," they called. "It's a perfect night for a sleigh ride."

Heather ran to ask her mom and dad if she could go. They said it was all right with them, as long as she dressed warmly. So Heather bundled up in her thickest coat and muffler and raced out to the sleigh. Mrs. Creighton pulled her up into the back seat next to Willie.

"Here we go," shouted Mr. Creighton, flicking the reins.

The horses neighed and off they went. It was quite a sensation! Moonlight glittered over the snow and the cold air sent prickles over Heather's skin. Bare trees looked like bony hands sticking up out of the ground. Faster and faster they glided until Mr. Creighton yelled, "Whoaaa! Hold up there, horses!"

But the horses did not slow down. They reared in the air and took off, running faster than before.

"Why won't they obey?" shouted Mrs. Creighton. "Hold on, kids!"

The trees and houses seemed to fly past. At first Heather was frightened, but then she noticed that Willie was smiling.

"Why are you smiling?" she asked.

"I'm not afraid of these horses," he said. "They just like to run sometimes. Close your eyes. Imagine that the sleigh is flying and that the horses are reindeer."

Heather shut her eyes and imagined flying over trees and rooftops.

Willie was right. It wasn't scary to go fast. It was fun! The horses were giving them the best ride ever.

Suddenly the sleigh stopped. Heather's eyes popped open. They had stopped next to a huge frozen lake.

"Come on," Heather yelled.

She jumped down from the sleigh and ran to the edge of the ice. She stomped her foot on it to make sure it was thick. It was. She slid out onto it and skidded on her snow boots.

Willie and Mr. and Mrs. Creighton were right behind her. Soon, everyone was slipping and sliding and scooting. Heather skated to the bank and scooped up a handful of wet snow. She made a big, soft snowball. When Willie slid by she threw it at him.

"You're in for it now," he said with a playful grin.

That started the game. A flurry of snowballs filled the air. Mr. and Mrs. Creighton joined in the fun until all four of them were powdered with snow.

    They looked like live snowmen skating back and forth. And all around them was the shimmer of moonlight over ice.

    When they were too tired to throw anymore, they got back in the sleigh and took off for home. The horses went wild again, running so fast that Mrs. Creighton covered her eyes with her hands. The horses' breath looked like steamy clouds.

    In no time at all, they arrived at Heather's house.

"My heart is beating fast," said Mrs. Creighton. "Horses give me a fright."

Willie winked at Heather, and she winked back.

"I think it was a great ride," said Heather, jumping down from the sleigh. "I'd like to go with you another time. Thank you very much."

Willie waved and Mrs. Creighton grabbed her hat as the horses raced home.

Heather ran inside. This was an adventure she would talk about for a long time.

ough

muff—   tough   rough   enough

            The meat was tough.

off—   cough   trough

            He had a terrible cough.

so—   dough   though   although   doughnut

            I'll go, although it is late.

cow— bough

The bird sat on the bough.

too— through

I saw her through the window.

taught— bought ought thought

Have you thought about what I said?

Did You Know?

Did you know that you can say
o-u-g-h in six ways?

To learn the six ways in no time,
You should read this little rhyme.

These are words I'll bet you know:
Though, although, and also *dough.*

And these words all sound like puff:
Enough and *rough*—They're not
 so *tough!*

Four more words will now be taught:
Bought and *brought,* and *thought*
    and *ought.*

And now some words we can't leave off:
A horse may *cough* at a water *trough.*

Can you imagine a purple cow
Sitting in a high tree *bough?*

Don't give up, don't be blue—
After this, our poem is *through!*

                Peg Chagnon

School Under the Trees

Freddie Applegate was eight years old and in the third grade. One afternoon his little sister Judy came home from school looking worried.

"What's the trouble?" asked Freddie.

"In reading, we're learning about the letters *o-u-g-h*," replied Judy.

"Well?" said Freddie.

"Well, I can't remember all the sounds those letters spell," said Judy.

"Don't be upset," said Freddie. "I couldn't keep them all straight at first either. But believe me, you'll learn all six of them in time."

But Judy still looked upset.

"Would you like me to help you?" asked Freddie. "I could pretend to be your teacher. We could have our lesson outside under the trees."

"That would be great!" replied Judy.

"I'll get everything we need," said

Freddie. "You can go and find some other students for our class."

Freddie hurried to the cellar where he made a great commotion. When he came back up, he had an old chalkboard, some chalk, and an eraser. He set up the chalkboard on the grass under a shady oak tree.

Just then Judy returned with two neighbors, Bonnie Wright and Earl Stephano. "Bonnie and Earl had trouble with *o-u-g-h* in school today, too," explained Judy. "So I asked them to join our class."

"Hi, Bonnie. Hi, Earl," called Freddie. "Have a seat in my schoolroom." Bonnie, Earl, and Judy sat on the grass.

"OK, class," said Freddie. "Let's get started. Who can spell the word *muff?*"

Earl raised his hand and said, "*Muff, m-u-f-f* spells *muff.*"

"Very good," said Freddie. "Now how do you spell *tough?*"

Earl held up his right arm to show how strong he was. "That's easy," he said. *"T-u-f-f* spells *tough."*

"Not quite," said Freddie. *Tough* rhymes with *muff*, but is not spelled the same way. Remember, words are not always spelled the way they sound."

Freddie took his piece of chalk and wrote **tough** on the chalkboard.

"Is that really the way it's spelled?" asked Earl.

"Yes," answered Freddie. "Here are some other words that rhyme with *muff*." Under **tough**, he wrote **rough** and **enough**.

Earl read the words, making each one rhyme with *muff*.

Then Freddie said, "Did you know that words ending in *o-u-g-h* can also rhyme with *off?* Now who can read this word? It is something people do when they have a cold."

"It must be *cough*," said Judy. "But it looks funny."

Then under **cough**, Freddie wrote **trough**. Bonnie read the words out loud—"*cough, trough*. What in the world is a *trough?*" she asked.

"A trough," replied Freddie, "is a long, narrow container for holding food or water. Some animals drink from a trough." Freddie drew a funny picture of a horse drinking from a trough.

Judy, Earl, and Bonnie laughed. They were starting to enjoy the lesson. Then Earl asked, "What other words can you spell with *o-u-g-h?*" He hoped Freddie would draw some more funny pictures.

"Sometimes *o-u-g-h* rhymes with *so*."

Freddie wrote **dough** on the board. "Who can read this word?" he asked.

Bonnie read the word *dough* out loud. "I know that word," she said "That's what bread is made from."

"Right," said Freddie. "And now that you know *dough*, you can read all these words, too." Under **dough**, he wrote **though**, **although**, and **doughnut**.

"Ummmmmm," said Earl, "reading about doughnuts is making me hungry."

"Here's a tricky one for you," said Freddie. "This word rhymes with *cow*. He wrote **bough** on the chalkboard.

"It must be *bough*," said Judy. "Bough-wow, bough-wow," shrieked Judy.

"No, no, no," replied Freddie. "That's **b-o-w**. Spelled **b-o-u-g-h** it means the limb of a tree."

"The next word rhymes with *to*," said Freddie. Under the word *to*, he wrote **throug**h.

"The word is *through*," said Judy.

"How did you know that?" asked Freddie.

"I was reading *Little Red Riding Hood* today," answered Judy, smiling. "Little Red Riding Hood went *through* the woods to her grandmother's house."

Freddie rolled his eyes.

"There's just one more sound that is spelled *o-u-g-h*," said Freddie. "I'm going to say a sentence with one word missing. The missing word rhymes with **taught**. Pearl went to the store and _____ a new sweater."

"Bought!" said Earl.

"Correct!" said Freddie. Then he wrote **bought**, **ought**, and **thought** on the chalkboard.

"Well," said Freddie, "those are the six different sounds the letters *o-u-g-h* spell." Then he took a bow.

The students clapped and cheered.

"Thanks for helping us," said Judy.

"Thanks, teacher," cried Bonnie and Earl.

"I know that was a *tough* lesson," said Freddie. "We're all *through* now, *though*. I *thought* you did very well. You deserve to sit under that *bough* over there and take a juice and *doughnut* break."

"What a clever brother I have," said Judy, as she rolled her eyes.

y as short i

| myth | mystery | physics | physician |
| physical | typical | symbol | rhythm |

uy as long i

| guy | buy | buyer | buying |

ui as long i

| guide | guided | guiding | disguise |

ui as short i

| build | building | built | guilty |

The Library

It looks like any building
When you pass it on the street,
Made of stone and glass and marble,
Made of iron and concrete.

But once inside you can ride
A camel or a train,
Visit Rome, Siam, or Nome,
Feel a hurricane,
Meet a king, learn to sing,
How to bake a pie,
Go to sea, plant a tree,
Find how airplanes fly,

Train a horse, and of course
Have all the dogs you'd like,
See the moon, a sandy dune,
Or catch a whopping pike.
Everything that books can bring
You'll find inside those walls.
A world is there for you to share
When adventure calls.

You cannot tell its magic
By the way the building looks,
But there's wonderment within it,
The wonderment of books.

Barbara A. Huff

Guy the Bookworm

Guy is not your typical everyday worm. Guy is a bookworm who grew up in a public library. His parents had settled on a shelf among the encyclopedias. Guy and his family spent all their time wandering through the encyclopedias from **A** to **Z**.

One day Guy decided he wanted to see the world. He wanted some real adventure.

Guy knew that no one was allowed to take encyclopedias from the library. If he stayed in the encyclopedias, he would never get to see the world. He would have to move.

So one bright spring day Guy began to inch his way along the shelves. He inched slowly past the encyclopedias. At last he came to rest in a book on crafts. He was tired.

"Finding adventure is hard work," Guy said to himself. Guy wiggled through the pages until he came to *quilts*. He settled down for a snooze.

Guy awakened with a start. The book was moving. *He* was moving! His adventure had begun!

The book stopped at the check-out desk. He heard a person say that his class would enjoy this book. Guy decided that a teacher was checking him out.

Guy spent many days in the teacher's classroom. Children picked up the book and looked through its pages.

He got to know a few of the children pretty well. But he hoped this was not going to be the end of his adventure.

Once a boy named Rudolph Tyler picked up the book and started to shake it. Guy had a terrific headache and an upset stomach from all that shaking. Guy decided he didn't like Rudolph.

One day, Guy heard the teacher ask Audrey to return the book to the library.

Back to the same old shelves, thought Guy. He stuck his head out of the book. He and Audrey were getting on a bus! His luck had changed.

Wow, thought Guy, *this is my first bus ride. This should be a real adventure.*

Audrey saw her friend Cecil on the bus. A few stops later Audrey and Cecil got off, but Audrey forgot to take the book. Guy and the book were left on the seat.

"Wait, you forgot me," shouted Guy in his loudest voice. But Guy's loudest voice was not loud enough, and no one heard him.

Then a lady boarded the bus and started to sit down on the seat.

"Watch out," Guy shouted, "you're going to sit on me!" But the lady stopped just in time. She picked up the book and started to look through the pages.

"It's a library book," she said. "Someone must have forgotten it. I'll take it back to the library myself."

But first the lady had to stop at the market to buy food for dinner. She put the book in the cart and bought what she needed. At the check-out counter she picked up her bags and left.

"Hey, lady," called Guy. "Wait!" But Guy had been forgotten again. Guy thought he would never get to see the rest of the world.

Before long, a teenager came to the market. He saw the book in the empty cart and picked it up. He held a radio in one arm and he put the book under his other arm. Guy moved his small body to the rhythm of the music.

All of a sudden the music stopped. Guy peeked out of the book. He found himself back at the library.

But wait a minute, Guy thought, *this is a different building. This library is much larger.*

Guy scrambled across the librarian's desk. He had enjoyed his adventures so far. He must find another book right away—a book someone was sure to check out.

Guy remembered that once a librarian had said many people liked mysteries. He crawled and crawled until he found the mystery books. Guy began to shudder as he read some of the titles—*The Legend of Sleepy Hollow*, the *Mystery of the Headless Horseman*.

Finally he found a title that didn't seem too scary. He crawled into *The Mixed-Up Mystery Smell*. He hoped he would not have to wait too long before someone checked him out.

Guy soon received his wish. A young girl was checking him out of the library. Guy was excited. He could hardly wait to see where she would take him.

Maybe Guy would get to see the world after all. What do you think?

Books on Wheels

"You know what?" said Barbara to her closest and best friend Tiffany.

"What?" asked Tiffany.

"The bookmobile is coming to our neighborhood."

"Yippee!" shouted Tiffany. "When will it be here? I want to get a good mystery book."

"It's coming this afternoon," said Barbara. "I heard that the bookmobile will be parked at the corner of Bridge and Meadow Streets."

Just then Barbara felt her little brother Marvin tugging on her sweater.

"What's a bookmobile?" he asked.

Little brothers can be pests sometimes, Barbara thought.

"Remember when Mom took us to that building with all the books?"

Marvin nodded his head.

"That was a library. And a bookmobile is a library, too."

"But it's a library on wheels," added Tiffany.

"You mean the books have wheels?" asked Marvin.

"No, not the books—the library," said Barbara. "A bookmobile is like a small van with all types of books inside. Our neighborhood doesn't have a library close by, so the bookmobile is coming."

"May I come with you?" asked Marvin.

"Sure," said Barbara. "You don't have a library card yet, but I'll check out a book for you."

"What kinds of books do you like, Marvin?" asked Tiffany.

"I like all kinds," replied Marvin. "But I already know which book I want. I want *Goldilocks and the Three Pigs*."

Tiffany and Barbara started to laugh. Marvin looked at both of them with a puzzled expression on his face.

Between giggles, Barbara said, "I think you are a little confused. But so you can get it straight, I'll check out *Goldilocks and the Three Bears* **and** *The Three Little Pigs*."

ai

captain   mountain   fountain
curtain   certain

ue

guess   guesses   guest   guests

ile

fertile   missile

silent t

fasten	often	listen	glisten
castle	thistle	whistle	trestle

silent n

hymn	column	solemn
autumn		

She'll Be Comin' 'Round the Mountain

She'll be comin' 'round the mountain
when she comes,
She'll be comin' 'round the mountain
when she comes,
She'll be comin' 'round the mountain,
She'll be comin' 'round the mountain,
She'll be comin' 'round the mountain
when she comes.

Oh, we'll listen for her whistle when she comes,
Oh, we'll listen for her whistle when she comes,
Oh, we'll listen for her whistle,
Oh, we'll listen for her whistle,
Oh, we'll listen for her whistle when she comes.

Oh, she'll clatter 'cross the trestle when she comes,
Oh, she'll clatter 'cross the trestle when she comes,
Oh, she'll clatter 'cross the trestle,
Oh, she'll clatter 'cross the trestle,
Oh, she'll clatter 'cross the trestle when she comes.

Oh, her red caboose will glisten when she comes,
Oh, her red caboose will glisten when she comes,
Oh, her red caboose will glisten,
Oh, her red caboose will glisten,
Oh, her red caboose will glisten when she comes.

Oh, the autumn leaves will rustle when she comes,
Oh, the autumn leaves will rustle when she comes,
Oh, the autumn leaves will rustle,
Oh, the autumn leaves will rustle,
Oh, the autumn leaves will rustle when she comes.

There will be no solemn faces when she comes,
There will be no solemn faces when she comes,
There will be no solemn faces,
There will be no solemn faces,
There will be no solemn faces when she comes.

The Hole in the Dike

A long time ago, a boy named Peter lived in Holland. He lived with his mother and father in a cottage next to a tulip field.

Peter loved to look at the bright tulips and the old windmills turning slowly.

He also enjoyed looking at the sea. In Holland the land is very low, and the sea is very high. The land is kept safe and dry by high, strong walls called *dikes*.

One day Peter went to join a friend who lived by the seaside.

Starting for home again, Peter saw that the sun was setting and the sky was growing dark. "I must hurry or I shall be late for supper," he said.

"Take the short-cut along the top of the dike," his friend called.

Peter wheeled his bike to the road on top of the dike. It had rained for several days, and the water was much higher than usual.

Peter thought, *It's lucky that the dikes are high and strong. Without these dikes, Holland would surely be flooded. Then everything would be washed away.*

Suddenly Peter heard a soft, gurgling noise. He saw a small stream of water trickling through a hole in the dike down below him.

Peter jumped off his bike to see what was wrong.

He couldn't believe his eyes. There in the big, strong dike was a leak!

Peter slid down the side of the dike. He stood up and tried putting his finger in the hole. It stopped most of the water from coming through!

Peter looked around for help, but he couldn't see anyone on the road. *Maybe if I shout,* he thought, *someone in the nearby field will hear me.*

He called out in a loud voice. But only his echo answered. Everyone had gone home.

Peter knew that if he let the water leak through the hole in the dike, the hole would get bigger and bigger. Then the sea would come gushing through. The fields and the houses and the windmills would all be flooded.

Peter looked around for something to plug up the leak so he could go to the village for help.

He put a stone in the hole, then a stick. But the stone and the stick were pushed out by the water.

Peter had no choice but to stay there alone. He had to use all his strength to keep the water from coming through.

From time to time he called for help. But no one heard him.

All night long Peter kept his finger in the dike. His finger and his hand grew cold and numb. He wanted to sleep, but he couldn't give up.

At last, early in the morning, Peter heard a welcome sound. Someone was coming! It was the milk cart noisily rumbling down the road.

Peter shouted for help. The milkman was surprised to hear someone's voice so early in the morning. He stopped and looked around.

"HELP!!" Peter shouted. "Here I am, at the bottom of the dike. There's a leak in the dike. Help! Help!"

The man saw Peter and hurried down to him. Peter pointed to the little stream of water still coming through.

Peter asked the milkman to hurry to the village. "Tell the people about the leak. Ask them to send some men to repair the dike right away!" he begged.

The milkman went as fast as he could. Peter stayed and kept his finger in the dike.

At last the men from the village came. They quickly set to work to repair the leak.

All the people thanked Peter and rejoiced. They carried him on their shoulders, shouting, "Make way for the hero of Holland! Peter is the brave and loyal boy who saved our land!"

But Peter did not think of himself as a hero. He had done what he thought was right. He was glad he could do something for Holland, the beautiful country he loved so much.

The Turtle Who Wanted to Fly

Characters

Narrator 1   Turtle
Narrator 2   Farmer
Pigeon 1   Boy
Pigeon 2   Wife

(Turtle may be a boy or a girl)

Prop List:

(These things can be either real or make-believe.)
feathers that can be pulled off Pigeons and stuck onto Turtle
a piece of rope
cornstalks

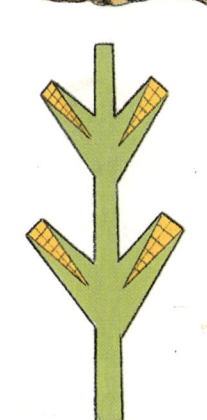

NARRATOR 1: There was once a turtle who was a dreamer. He couldn't run very fast. And he couldn't swim very far. He couldn't draw very well. But he could sing just beautifully.

(TURTLE *enters singing a tune without words.*)

NARRATOR 2: And because he could sing very well, he would sing for hours every day. Sometimes he would sing about things he liked. (TURTLE *sings to himself a little song about things he likes.*)

NARRATOR 1: And sometimes he would sing about things he didn't like.

(TURTLE *sings a little song to himself about things he hates.*)

NARRATOR 2: But mostly he would sing about things he wished he could do.

TURTLE: *(while singing, tries to do these actions)*

I wish I could swim like a green crocodile.
I wish I could run like a long-legged deer.
I wish I could swing from my tail like a monkey.
And, if I try hard enough,
And, if I try hard enough,
And, if I try hard enough,
   you can never tell,
   you can never tell,
If I try hard enough,
   perhaps I could do it!

NARRATOR 1: But what he really wanted to do more than anything else was to fly. (PIGEONS *fly in a circle around the stage.* TURTLE *stops singing and watches them in awe.*)

TURTLE: Oh, I wish I could fly. I wish I could fly more than anything else in the world. If I could take up flying, I'd even give up singing. Yes, gladly. (PIGEONS *fly by again.*)

TURTLE: Birds! Pigeons! Please come here. I want to talk to you, but I can't go that fast. (*Both* PIGEONS *pause.*)

PIGEON 1: Hello there, Turtle.

PIGEON 2: Hello, friend. We thought we heard you singing as we flew by.

PIGEON 1: It sounded beautiful. It makes me feel like flying.

PIGEON 2: Would you mind singing another little tune right now?

TURTLE: Yes, I'll sing a verse or two.

(*He sings his little tune.*)

(*PIGEONS dance-fly until TURTLE stops singing.*)

PIGEON 1: That was marvelous.

PIGEON 2: When you sing, it makes me feel like dancing-flying.

TURTLE: Oh, thank you. It makes me feel like flying, too. In fact, I always feel like flying. But I can't. I've tried and tried but I just can't do it. Would you watch me? Maybe you can tell what I'm doing wrong.

(PIGEONS *watch while* TURTLE *tries to move his flippers and feet; his shell makes it very hard to do.*)

PIGEON 3: You are trying hard enough . . .

PIGEON 4: . . . But it will never work. If you ask me, it's because you have no feathers.

PIGEON 1: Feathers! Why, at planting time when I lost all my feathers...

PIGEON 2: ...you couldn't fly a bit.

PIGEON 1: Right. I had to wait till they all grew in again.

TURTLE: Feathers! I've never had any feathers. I don't think I'll ever grow any either, because I've been waiting to fly for a long time and not a single feather has grown.

PIGEON 2: Look, I'll give you a few of mine. I don't need every last one.

PIGEON 1: I can spare some, too. I'd like to help you out with this because I certainly do like it when you sing. (PIGEONS *pull feathers from their wings and stick them in* TURTLE'S *shell.*)

TURTLE: *(growing more excited as each feather is added)* I'm beautiful! Oh, look, how beautiful I am! *(He spins around to show feathers.)* I feel all dressed up with no place to go. Where shall we fly?

PIGEON 1: We were just on our way to the corn field over there. Come along with us, and we'll have a corn feast to celebrate.

(PIGEONS *fly to the far side of the stage, and* TURTLE *follows clumsily. He is so excited by the feathers that he really believes his walking is flying.*)

TURTLE: This is wonderful. I am flying! I am just like one of the pigeons.

PIGEON 2: The corn is much better than it was last week.

PIGEON 1: *(speaking to TURTLE)* Are you enjoying it, friend?

TURTLE: Oh ... yes, it's delicious.

PIGEON 1: *(moving to a new place for more corn, notices something off-stage)* Quick! Fly. I see the farmer coming.

PIGEON 2: *(darting over to look)* His boy is with him, too. Get out fast.

PIGEON 2: They killed two crows last week. Hurry up.

PIGEON 1: Come on! Fly. Fly. *(The two PIGEONS exit.)*

TURTLE: I'm coming. Don't wait. I can't fly as fast as you can. I'll catch up in a minute.

(TURTLE *tries to fly. He flaps his flippers very hard but, of course, goes nowhere.* FARMER AND BOY *enter, see him;* FARMER *signals to* BOY *to grab* TURTLE. *But* BOY *is so full of fun and silliness that* FARMER'S *commands don't get through to him.*)

FARMER: Get him.
   (*They do a funny mix-up here with* BOY *grabbing* FARMER, *who then throws him off. Each grabs for a flipper, but* TURTLE *quickly pulls flippers into his shell.* FARMER *finally seizes* TURTLE *by the neck.*)
FARMER: I've got him. Go get a rope.
   (BOY *dashes off to get it.*)

FARMER: We can have stewed turtle with our corn tonight. (BOY *dashes back quickly with a rope.*)

TURTLE: I'm not a turtle. I'm a bird.

FARMER: You look like a turtle to me.
(*They put a rope around his back.*)

TURTLE: Well, I'm a flying turtle.

BOY: Then why didn't you fly?

TURTLE: (*hurt by the truth*) Oh . . .
(FARMER *and* BOY *start to walk home, leading the turtle by the rope.*)

NARRATOR 2: The turtle was upset but he realized this was no time for just wishing. So he said to himself:

TURTLE: Things being what they are, I think I'd better give up flying and take up singing.

(TURTLE *starts to sing, and* FARMER *and* BOY *begin to sway and dance until they get themselves and* TURTLE *all tangled up.*

(TURTLE *stops singing.*)

FARMER: Now, look what you have done!

BOY: It wasn't my fault. You were dancing, too.

FARMER: Never mind about that. Get me untangled. (BOY *makes it worse.*) No, the other way. *(They get straightened out.)* I'll take the turtle home; you get the corn. (BOY *scrambles off.)*

FARMER: Wife, here is a surprise for you. We caught a turtle for supper. Please start to cook him in your special sauce while I go help our boy get the corn.

TURTLE: Oh. (*shrinks into shell.*)

(FARMER *and* WIFE *look surprised.*)

WIFE: Gladly. This is a treat. He'll be ready to eat by the time you get back. (FARMER *leaves and* WIFE *prepares to go to work.* WIFE *is puzzled as she looks* TURTLE *over.*) What a strange-looking creature you are, covered with feathers. Shall I cook you like a bird or like a turtle?

NARRATOR 1: The turtle felt he'd better speak up, so he said:

TURTLE: I think I'm better as a turtle. You could pluck off my feathers, and I'll look exactly like a turtle again.

WIFE: Thank you for your suggestion. It's a good idea. (*She starts to remove his feathers.*)

NARRATOR 2: As the feathers were removed, the turtle began to feel like himself again. This cheered him up a lot, and he began to sing softly. (TURTLE *begins to sing.*) Can you guess what happened this time? *(The* WIFE *begins to dance.)*

NARRATOR 1: When the turtle saw what was happening, he sang all the louder. He sang and sang. The farmer returned and said:

FARMER: *(enters followed by* BOY *with corn)* Why, that turtle isn't ready! What is this dancing here? *(He tries to stop his* WIFE, *but he is also overcome by* TURTLE'S *singing and joins in dancing, as does* BOY.)

NARRATOR 2: But the turtle kept on singing, and the farmer and his family danced and danced. They never even noticed that the turtle's friend had come to find him.

PIGEON 1: *(flies on)* Come on quickly. *(motions to* TURTLE*)* Follow me. *(Still singing,* TURTLE *happily hurries off stage after* PIGEON.*)*

NARRATOR 1: And the turtle sang very loudly and walked very quietly until he was out of sight. *(*FARMER, WIFE, *and* BOY *dance off in other direction.)*

It's a Small World

It's a world of laughter, a world of tears;
it's a world of hopes and a world of fears.
There's so much that we share that it's time we're aware.
It's a small world after all.

It's a small world after all,
It's a small world after all,
It's a small world after all,
It's a small, small world.

There is just one moon and one golden
   sun,
and a smile means friendship to
   everyone.
Though the mountains divide and the
   oceans are wide,
It's a small world after all.

"IT'S A SMALL WORLD" Words & Music by: Richard M. & Robert B. Sherman. Copyright © 1963 Wonderland Music Company, Inc.

The Chef's Party

Louis was the best chef in the city. His recipes for sourdough bread, oyster chowder, and lemon chiffon pie brought folks to his place from miles around.

One day Louis was asked to cater a party at a mansion. It was an important job! He and his helpers kneaded the dough, cut up the oysters with knives, and whipped the eggs for the chiffon pie. When they were through, there was enough food to feed an army.

They loaded it all into the back of a truck and started to drive to the party. The streets were crowded with cars, and Louis knew they would be late if they went this slowly.

"We have to hurry!" he complained.

They were passing a park when he saw a gap in the traffic. He stepped on the gas. The truck jolted forward too fast and smashed into a telephone pole!

Folks came running to the wreck.

"Is everyone all right?" they shouted.

Louis looked around at his helpers. They were dizzy, though no one was hurt. But the food was a mess! It had slid off the back of the truck and into the park.

Long loaves of sourdough were scattered like logs. Puddles of chowder steamed in the grass. Lemon chiffon pie was dripping down the tree trunks. Louis sat on the curb holding his head and rocking backward and forward.

"What a disaster!" he moaned. "The party is going on at the mansion, but there will be no food."

Then he heard laughter and lips smacking. He looked up to find folks from all over the park eating his food. They were picking up bread and slurping chowder from the grass. They were scooping chiffon pie from the trees.

"Don't fret, Louis," said one helper with chiffon pie all over his cheeks. "Call the mansion and tell them about the wreck. They should understand. Invite them to come and join our party. We can't let all this delicious food go to waste."

"Ok. I'll be right back," yelled Louis.

Louis stood up and ran to a phone booth down the street. He called the folks at the mansion.

"Where is our food?" demanded the man who had hired Louis. "You are very late and all our stomachs are growling!"

"I'm so sorry," said Louis. "We had a wreck near the park and the food spilled everywhere."

"A wreck?" said the man. "How awful! Was anyone hurt?"

"No. Everyone is fine," said Louis. "But we were wondering if *your* party would like to join *our* party down at the park. There is plenty of good food for everyone."

"That is a splendid idea!" said the man. "Now the day won't be a disaster after all! See you in about ten minutes."

Louis hung up the phone. He grinned and started back toward the park. The sound of smacking lips was getting louder and louder.

Eletelephony

Once there was an elephant,
Who tried to use the telephant—
No! No! I mean an elephone
Who tried to use the telephone—
(Dear me! I am not certain quite
That even now I've got it right.)

However it was, he got his trunk
Entangled in the telephunk;
The more he tried to get it free,
The louder buzzed the telephee—
(I fear I'd better drop the song
Of elephop and telephong!)

Laura E. Richards

The Muffin Muncher

Many, many years ago in the far corner of a very poor country stood the poorest of poor castles.

The only way the people had survived at all was by baking and selling the most delicious muffins in the land.

Every morning the king, who was also the head baker, would bake a fresh batch of muffins. When he had finished, the villagers would load their carts and set off for other villages in the kingdom.

There was never any problem selling the muffins since they were the finest ever baked. But because the villagers were so poor, they had to use all the money they had earned to buy more firewood and flour in order to make more muffins.

So, day in and day out, the head baker, who was also the king, would build up the giant fires in the ovens and bake muffins and muffins and muffins.

The villagers were just barely surviving. As if things weren't bad enough for them, there appeared at the castle one day a great and monstrous dragon. Now, this was not your everyday, run-of-the-mill dragon dragon. He was a rather enormous, slightly overweight, muffin-munching dragon.

With crumbs still on his face from the muffins he'd eaten at the last castle he'd visited, the dragon came trotting down the hill. He went right up to the drawbridge.

Taking one look at the dragon, the villagers quickly ran over the drawbridge and hurried into the castle to hide.

The dragon took a great, long sniff. "Ahh," he mumbled, "I smell muffins!" This castle, he decided, smelled like a nice place to stay.

The dragon picked up his suitcase and moved in, right under the drawbridge.

He was very tired from his long journey. So he unpacked his pillow, his pajamas, and the picture of his pony. Then he curled up, and fell fast asleep.

The next morning the villagers looked out of their castle windows and thought that the dragon was gone. Breathing a sigh of relief, they calmly began preparing for another day.

After loading their wagons with fresh, warm muffins, they set off across the drawbridge, over the soundly-sleeping dragon. With all the rattling from the wagons, the dragon awoke with a start.

He yawned once, stretched twice, and peeked over the edge to see what was going on. "So, that's it! Those muffins look so good, and I am so very hungry!"

He thought and thought and finally came up with a plan.

The dragon jumped onto the bridge and stood right in front of the villagers. He tried to look very ferocious. He roared loudly, "Stop, or I shall burn up your drawbridge!" Then, to be just a little more convincing, he blew a little flame and puffed three smoke rings.

"From now on," he rumbled, "you shall each give me ten of your most delicious muffins as your toll to cross my bridge."

"But this is our drawbridge!" they cried.

"Well, if I burn it up, it won't be anybody's drawbridge," said the dragon.

The villagers thought and talked for a moment and finally agreed to give the dragon his muffins. They barely had enough money to buy firewood, let alone enough wood to build a new drawbridge.

From then on, every wagon that crossed the drawbridge left the dragon ten delicious muffins. With crumbs all around him, the dragon would sit there, happily stuffing those scrumptious muffins into his mouth.

This probably would have gone on to this very day except for one slight problem. The dragon was eating so many muffins that the villagers did not have enough to sell. Because of that, they didn't have enough money to buy firewood for the ovens, or even enough flour to bake more muffins.

They would return every day with fewer and fewer supplies, until one day they all came home with nothing.

With a heavy heart and a tear in his eye, the head baker, who was also the king, sat sadly on a pile of empty flour sacks. He cried, "We have no more supplies to make muffins, and no more wood to light the fires. We cannot bake any more muffins, and the dragon will burn our drawbridge down. What are we ever to do?"

That very same day the dragon woke up, brushed his teeth, combed his hair, and prepared for another day of muffin munching.

He waited and waited and waited. No wagons came, no muffins came, and the dragon's stomach began to rumble, grumble, and growl.

Finally he decided to enter the castle and find out what had happened to all his muffins.

The dragon wandered through the castle until he reached the bakery. Then he peeked inside. "Where are my muffins?" he rumbled. "I've been waiting and waiting and waiting! **Where are my muffins?**"

The head baker, who was also the king, walked up to the dragon as bravely as he could. "Mr. Dragon," he said, "we are poor villagers, living in a poor castle which has very little. Before you came, the muffins we sold barely paid for our firewood and supplies. Now that we have to give you so many muffins, we can't afford to buy enough firewood. And our ovens have no heat."

The dragon thought and thought. Finally, a great big smile crossed his face. "I have it!" he shouted. He asked the head baker, who was also the king, to call all the villagers to the castle so that he could tell them of his marvelous plan.

Then and for always, the dragon heated the ovens of the bakery with his mighty flame. With the extra money they saved, the villagers could easily afford to leave a generous stack of muffins for the muffin-munching dragon.

While heating up the ovens
With a lot of style and grace,
The muffin muncher smiles a smile
With crumbs upon his face.

The Terrible Thing That Happened at Our House

My mother used to be a real mother. In the morning, when my brother and I left for school, she'd kiss us and wave good-bye.

"Have a nice day, darling. Be good, honey," she'd say as we went out the door.

When we came home for lunch, we'd have toasted cheese sandwiches or tuna on a bun. Then we would have chocolate pudding or a cupcake for dessert—with sprinkles on top.

After school she'd listen to us tell about who got punched in the stomach, or what happened to Abby on the stairs. She'd even listen to me explain how the teacher yelled when I dropped my box of colored markers all over the floor. Then she'd pour us a glass of milk and give us a snack.

Afterwards we'd go outside or have friends come and play at our house. My mother always had time to read to us and help us make things and take us to the park.

BUT THEN SOMETHING TERRIBLE HAPPENED TO CHANGE ALL THAT.

My mother went back to being a science teacher. She said it was important work. I always thought taking care of us was pretty important. But she said we could do a lot more for ourselves than we did.

That's when everything began to be different. In the mornings we had to rush around making our own beds and clearing the table. We had to do this because my mother was busy getting ready to leave, too. We even had to find our own underwear and socks.

We had to eat lunch in school because there was no one home at lunchtime anymore.

I HATE EATING LUNCH IN SCHOOL. The lunchroom smells like fish or frankfurters . . . And all that yelling gave me a headache.

After school, instead of listening to us the way she used to, my mother would say, "I need a few minutes to clear my head, kids—I've had a really tough day." I told her how the teacher kept me in at recess just because I sharpened my pencil three times during math. She said, "You must have been annoying her, dear," instead of being on my side.

My father used to be a real father, too. He'd come home from work and say, "Hi, everybody—what's for dinner?" Then he'd listen to my brother and me talk while he washed up and changed. He told us things about his office or about what happened on the way to work.

When we finished eating dinner, he'd clear the table while my brother and I did our homework or watched TV. And later, maybe he'd have time for a game. My father used to read us stories every night before we went to bed. But that's all different now, too.

My father began coming home with packages from the supermarket. "I'll get dinner tonight," he'd say. And then he'd tell us we were having frozen salmon croquettes or meatballs in wine sauce.

I HATE SALMON CROQUETTES AND MEATBALLS IN WINE SAUCE. They smell like what we have for lunch in school. Yichhhhh!

My brother and I had to clear the table after dinner while my father did the dishes with my mother. Sometimes he did them all by himself while she marked tests or planned tomorrow's lesson in the living room. And half the time he didn't read us stories, because he was too busy helping to fold laundry.

I tried reading to my brother, but he picked boring books and asked dumb questions.

My parents said we were all much happier now.

Then, one night at dinner my brother kept talking and talking. No one was really listening to him or even heard me when I asked for more milk. I got mad. I got so mad I started yelling.

NO ONE CARES ANYMORE IN THIS HOUSE. NO ONE LISTENS. NO ONE HELPS YOU. NO ONE EVEN PASSES THE MILK WHEN YOU NEED IT!

Everyone stopped talking and looked at me. My mother said, "Oh, you poor thing," and came and put her arms around me.

My father said, "What's bothering you, sweetheart?"

And my brother passed me the milk.

I told them how I couldn't stand all this rushing around every morning. And how I hated eating lunch in school. And how no one had time to hear what happened to me during the day. And how I was sick and tired of missing stories and talks and games and everything.

My parents really listened this time and then they said, "Let's see what we can do."

They decided that if we all got up a little bit earlier, and my father left for work a little bit later, we could get out in the morning without so much rushing.

My mother asked Louisa, who lives next door, if we could eat lunch at home with her kids. She said, "Sure," except on Fridays when she goes to get her allergy shots.

And Ellen, our babysitter, began to come for an hour after school. Now my mother has a little time to herself for clearing her head or reading the mail or doing the wash.

Some afternoons we help to dust, or just pick up. Then she feels more like making things with us, or walking to the park.

My brother and I said we could fold the laundry so my father would have time to read us a story. The socks don't always come out right, but we're getting better.

We take turns choosing what to have for supper. Sometimes I go to the supermarket with my father. My mother is teaching my brother and me how to make hamburgers . . . the plain kind.

After we clean up in the kitchen and get our work done, most nights there's still time to play a game or talk together.

Things aren't so terrible at our house anymore. I guess they're a real mother and father after all.

Jonathan George

Jonathan George was sick with the flu;
Jonathan George had nothing to do.
His big brother Bill asked him, "Why don't we play?
Let's think of the shapes that we see every day."

Jonathan George said, "That sounds like fun—
But what is a shape? Please, do tell me one."

Bill answered. "Well, there's a circle, a square,
And a triangle, too. There are shapes everywhere.

"A circle, you know, just keeps going around—
Like my bicycle wheels spinning over the ground.

"Buttons are circles; we see lots of those,
Like the bright silver ones on my new Sunday clothes.

"There are circles of honey that drip from my toast.
And doughnuts are circles that I like the most!

"The bubbles that dance from my wand in the sun,
And Mom's silly glasses she wears just for fun,

"The shiny new penny I keep in my shoe,
The green lollipop that I bought just for you,

"The big, bouncing ball that we use when we play—
All these things are circles we see every day.

"A triangle has three straight sides, I can tell—
Like the top of our church that houses the bell.

"A triangle's a piece of a blueberry pie,
And the top of my rocket that shoots toward the sky.

"It's the sail on my boat, with bright stripes of red,
And the newspaper hat that I wear on my head.

"Some fishes' tails and some butterfly wings
Are some of the prettier triangle things.

"The shade on my lamp and half of my tie
Are two other triangle things that I spy.

The top half of my kite and the bottom half, too.
Are each a triangle way up in the blue.

"Four sides make a square; that's how it is built—
Like each of the patches that makes up my quilt.
"There are pink squares that cover our whole bathroom wall;
Our windows are glass squares—and that is not all—

"The box of my treasures I keep in my drawer,
The blue tiles all over our dining room floor,

"The sections of sidewalk in our neighborhood,
The crispy graham crackers that always taste good,

"The alphabet blocks that are printed so gay—
All these things are squares that we see every day.

"Squares make a waffle; some squares make a book.
There seem to be squares wherever I look!"

Jonathan George is still sick with
  the flu—
But Jonathan George has plenty to do.

He's looking for shapes all over—and
  then,
Before very long, he'll be all well again!

The Goat in the Rug

My name is Geraldine. I live near a place called Window Rock with my friend, Glenmae. She is a Navajo weaver.

Glenmae is called Glenmae most of the time because it's easier to say than her Indian name: Glee 'Nasbah.

One day, Glenmae decided to weave me into a rug. I remember it was a warm, sunny afternoon.

Glenmae had spent most of the morning sharpening a large pair of scissors. I had no idea what she was going to use them for, but it didn't take me long to find out.

Before I knew what was happening, I was on the ground and Glenmae was clipping off my wool in great long strands. It didn't hurt at all, but I admit I kicked up my heels some. I'm very ticklish for a goat.

I might have looked a little naked and silly afterwards, but my, did I feel nice and cool.

So I decided to stick around and see what would happen next.

The first thing Glenmae did was chop up roots from a yucca plant. The roots made a soapy, rich lather when she mixed them with water.

She washed my wool in the suds until it was clean and white.

After that, a little bit of me (you might say) was hung up in the sun to dry. When my wool was dry, Glenmae took out two large square combs with teeth in them.

By combing my wool between these combs, she removed any bits of twigs or burrs and straightened out the fibers. She told me it helped make a smoother yarn for spinning.

Then Glenmae carefully started to spin my wool into yarn. I was beginning to find out it takes a long while to make a Navajo rug.

Again and again, Glenmae twisted and pulled the wool. Then she spun it around a long, thin stick she called a spindle. As she twisted and pulled and spun, the yarn became finer, stronger, and smoother.

A few days later, Glenmae and I went for a walk. She said we were going to find some special plants she would use to make dye.

I didn't know what "dye" meant, but it sounded like a picnic to me. I do love to eat plants. That's what got me into trouble.

While Glenmae was out looking for more plants, I ate every one she had already collected in her bucket. Delicious!

    The next day, Glenmae made me stay home while she walked miles to a store. She said the dye she could buy wasn't the same as the kind she makes from plants. But since I'd made such a pig of myself, it would have to do.

    I was really worried that she would still be angry with me when she got back. She wasn't, though, and pretty soon she had three big potfuls of dye boiling over a fire.

Then I saw what Glenmae had meant by dyeing. She dipped my white wool into one pot . . . and it turned pink! She dipped it in again. It turned a darker pink! By the time she'd finished dipping it in and out and hung it up to dry, it was a beautiful deep red.

After that, she dyed some of my wool brown, and some of it black. I couldn't help wondering if those plants I'd eaten would turn me the same colors.

While I was worrying about that, Glenmae started to make our rug. She took a ball of yarn and wrapped it around two poles. I lost count when she'd reached three hundred wraps. I guess I was too busy thinking about what it would be like to be the only red, white, black, and brown goat at Window Rock.

It wasn't long before Glenmae had finished wrapping. Then she hung the

poles with the yarn on a big wooden frame. It looked like a picture frame made of logs—she called it a "loom."

After a whole week of getting ready to weave, Glenmae started. She began weaving at the bottom of the loom. Then, one strand of yarn at a time, our rug started growing toward the top.

A few strands of black.

A few of brown.

A few of red.

In and out. Back and forth.

Until in a few days, the pattern of our rug was clear to see.

Our rug grew very slowly. Like all Navajo weavers before her, Glenmae formed her own design. This design would be different from all others.

Then, at last, the weaving was finished! But not until I'd checked it quite thoroughly in front . . . and in back. Then I let Glenmae take our rug off the loom.

There was a lot of me in that rug. I wanted it to be perfect. It was.

Since then, my wool has grown almost long enough for Glenmae and me to make another rug. I hope we do very soon. Because, you see, there aren't too many weavers like Glenmae left among the Navajos.

And there's only one goat like me, Geraldine.

Every Time I Climb a Tree

Every time I climb a tree
Every time I climb a tree
Every time I climb a tree
I scrape a leg
Or skin a knee
And every time I climb a tree
I find some ants
Or dodge a bee
And get the ants
All over me.

And every time I climb a tree
Where have you been?
They say to me
But don't they know that I am free
Every time I climb a tree?
I like it best
To spot a nest
That has an egg
Or maybe three

And then I skin
The other leg
But every time I climb a tree
I see a lot of things to see
Swallows, rooftops, and TV,
And all the fields and farms there be
Every time I climb a tree
Though climbing may be good for ants
It isn't awfully good for pants
But still it's pretty good for me
Every time I climb a tree.

David McCord

Story Time

Gerald Orson Willis liked to tell stories into a tape recorder. Gerald didn't know it, but his machine was different. Because of a mistake at the tape-recorder factory, everything that was said into this tape recorder would come true.

One day Gerald began telling a story into the tape recorder. This is what he said:

A Martian named Xixobrax came to Earth and began to study it. The Martian wanted to take over the Earth, but he couldn't find out how to do it. So Xixobrax decided to ask an Earth person to help him.

Just then there was a knock at the door. When Gerald opened the door, his eyes almost popped out of his head. He couldn't say anything for a while, or even move. Gerald Orson Willis had never seen a real, live Martian before—at least not a Martian named Xixobrax!

The Martian clicked its claws at him and said, "Hello."

After a long time, Gerald finally said "Hello," too. He couldn't think of anything else to say. Xixobrax was bright green, and two and one-half meters tall (about eight feet). He had twelve brown eyes running down his body like coat buttons. The sight of all those eyes made Gerald very nervous.

"I don't know how to take over the Earth," the Martian said.

Gerald tried to stop shaking. "That's too bad," he said.

"You have to help me," said the Martian.

"Why?" Gerald asked.

"Because you made me up," the Martian said. "And because you made me want to take over the Earth. So now you have to tell me how." His eyes blinked on and off, one at a time, bottom to top.

Gerald Orson Willis was more nervous now than before. He believed that his story about a Martian taking over the Earth was a good one. But he never meant for it to come true. He asked, "What will happen to me if I don't help you?"

"Not much," the Martian said. "Except I'll stay here for as long as it takes. I don't believe you'd like that. I'm a peaceful Martian, but I do get hungry. And one of the things I like eating most is Earth people!"

Gerald sat down on the floor and tried to think. He had dreamed up the Martian for his story, and the Martian had come true. This meant that either there was something special about Gerald Orson Willis, or there was something special about his *tape recorder.*

To solve the mystery, Gerald turned on the machine. Then he said, "Xixobrax was holding a candy cane in one claw." All at once, a candy cane appeared in the Martian's right claw! Gerald turned the tape recorder *off*. Then he said, "In the other claw, the Martian was holding a bunch of daisies." Nothing happened this time. No daisies—nothing!

Xixobrax was looking at the candy cane. He was wondering if the candy cane was something to eat or a new secret weapon. Xixobrax could take over the Earth by saying, "Xixobrax took over the Earth," into the tape recorder. But the Martian didn't know that yet. Besides, he was too busy studying the candy cane.

Gerald could have told the tape recorder that Xixobrax didn't exist anymore. And Xixobrax would have disappeared. But instead, Gerald decided to ask the Martian a question. "Except for taking over the Earth, what do you really want?"

Xixobrax's eyes blinked on and off again, one at a time. (Martians do that when they think really hard.) "I'd like to go back to Mars," he said at last. "I'm happier there. And I'd like to take some of these things with me. He waved the candy cane in the air. "I get very hungry. And once I'm back on Mars, I won't be able to eat people anymore."

Before the Martian could find out the secret of the tape recorder, Gerald turned on the machine. Then he said, "Xixobrax went back to Mars, carrying 600 candy canes." To his relief, it worked! Covered with brand-new candy canes, the Martian disappeared.

Gerald took a deep breath and stared at the tape recorder. He knew that anything he said into it would come true. He thought about money, and travel, and gold, and candy canes. But he finally decided that he had done enough harm with the tape recorder. If he made anything else come true, it might be even worse. And he might have a much harder time fixing it up.

So Gerald Orson Willis did a very hard thing: he sold the tape recorder. Then he bought a new one . . . a normal one.

You probably think that Gerald Orson Willis did the right thing. But you're wrong! He should have destroyed the tape recorder. Or at least, he should have told it not to go on making things come true . . . because that tape recorder still exists—somewhere. And whatever a person says into the tape recorder is going to come true!

I don't know where it is anymore. That is why I'm telling you this story. Please, be careful what you say—the tape recorder might be listening!

Rumpelstiltskin

In a country a long way off, a fine stream of water ran along beside a wood. Next to the stream there stood a mill with the miller's house close by. The miller had a very beautiful daughter. She was also very shrewd and smart. The miller was very proud of his daughter. One day he was speaking to the king of the land. He boasted that his daughter was so clever that she could spin gold out of straw.

This king was very greedy. He said to the miller, "If indeed your daughter is as clever as you say, bring her to my castle tomorrow. I am most eager to see if what you say is true."

When the girl was brought to him, the king led her into a room that was quite full of straw. He gave her a wheel and a spindle.

"Now set to work," said the king. "All this straw must be spun into gold before morning or you shall die." Then the

king shut the door himself and left her there alone.

The poor miller's daughter sat down. She didn't know what in the world she was going to do. She hadn't the least idea of how to spin straw into gold. She became so miserable that she began to cry.

Then all at once the door opened. In came a little man.

"Good evening, miller's daughter," he said. "Why are you crying?"

"Oh!" sobbed the girl. "I have to spin gold out of straw, and I don't know how to do it."

"What will you give me if I spin it for you?" asked the little man.

"My necklace," replied the girl.

The little man took the necklace. He seated himself in front of the wheel. *Whir, whir, whir,* the wheel went round three times, and the bobbin was full. Then he put on another. *Whir, whir, whir,* the wheel went round three times, and the second bobbin was full. And so it went till the morning. All the straw was spun and all the bobbins were full of gold.

At sunrise the king came in. When he saw the gold, he rejoiced, for he was very greedy. He took the miller's daughter into another room filled with straw, much bigger than the last. He told her that if she wanted to save her life, she must spin it all in one night.

The girl did not know what to do. She began to cry. Then the door opened, and the little man appeared.

"What will you give me if I spin all this straw into gold for you?" he asked.

"The ring from my finger," answered the girl.

So the little man took the ring and began again to send the wheel whirring round. By the next morning all the straw was spun into shining gold.

Again the king rejoiced. Since he could never have enough gold, he took the miller's daughter into a still larger room full of straw.

"This, too, must be spun in one night," he said. "If you accomplish it, you shall be my wife."

As soon as the girl was left alone, the little man appeared for the third time.

"What will you give me if I spin the straw for you this time?" he asked.

"I have nothing left to give you," answered the girl.

"Then you must promise to give me the first child you have after you are queen," said the little man.

The girl did not know what else to do, so she promised the little man what he asked.

The little man began to spin until all the straw was gold.

When the king came in the morning, he found that all had been done according to his wish. He arranged for the wedding to be held at once. The miller's pretty daughter became the queen.

The following year, the queen brought a fine child into the world. She thought no more about the little man. But one day he suddenly came into her room.

"Now give me what you promised," he said.

The queen was frightened. She offered him all the riches of the kingdom if he would leave the child. But the little man said, "No, I would rather have something living than all the treasures of the world."

Then the queen began to weep. The little man had pity upon her.

"I will give you three days," he said. "If at the end of that time you cannot tell my name, you must give me the child."

The queen spent the whole night thinking about all the names that she had ever heard. She also sent a messenger through the land to ask far and wide for all the names that could be found.

When the little man came the next day, she repeated all the names she

knew beginning with Casper, Melchior, and Balthasar.

But after each name, the little man would answer nothing except: "That is not my name."

The second day the queen sent the messenger to ask for the names of all the neighbors and their servants. When the little man showed up, the queen tried even the most unusual names, saying:

"Perhaps you are called Roast-ribs, or Sheep-shanks, or Spindle-shanks?"

Each time the little man would answer nothing except:

"That is not my name."

The third day the messenger came back again. He said, "I have not been able to find one single new name. But as I passed through the woods, I came to a high hill. Near it was a little house, and in front of the house burned a fire. Round the fire danced a funny

little man. He hopped up and down on one leg and cried:

"Today do I bake, tomorrow I brew,
The day after that the queen's child comes in;
And oh! I am glad that nobody knew
That the name I am called is Rumpelstiltskin!"

You cannot think how pleased the queen was to hear that name. Soon afterwards, the little man walked in.

"Now, oh, Queen, what is my name?" he asked.

"Are you called Jack?" she asked.

"No," he answered.

"Are you called Harry?" she asked.

"No," he answered.

Then she said, "Perhaps your name is Rumpelstiltskin!"

"The devil told you that! The devil told you that!" cried the little man.

In his anger he stamped with his left foot so hard that it went into the ground above his knee. Then he seized his right foot with both his hands in such a fury that he split in two. And that was the end of Rumpelstiltskin.

Glossary

accomplish   carry out; finish or complete.
ac com' plish

achieve   1. finish something well; accomplish.   2. reach a goal: *I want to achieve good marks in school.*
a chieve'

afterwards   later: *We had a rest and afterwards we went swimming.*
af' ter wards

allergy   when a person's body cannot stand certain foods, plants, or other things that may not bother other people: *He has an allergy to wool.*
al' ler gy

annoy   bother; tease; make a little angry.
an noy'

autumn   the time of year between summer and winter; fall.
au' tumn

awe   great wonder: *He looked at the mountain in awe.*

batch   the amount of rolls, bread, muffins or cookies made at one baking.

bay   part of a sea or lake that comes into or meets the land.

block   1. wood, plastic, or foam in a square shape used as a toy: *She built a tall tower one block at a time.*   2. the distance from one street corner to the next; four streets that come together to make a square.   3. stop movement; get in the way: *Do not block the sidewalk with your bike.*

bobbin   spool for holding thread, string, or yarn.
bob' bin

bore   1. dull: *That show was boring.*   2. make tired by talking on and on.

box a container that is used to hold things.

brew make something to drink by mixing, boiling, and soaking.

brief short

bright shining; giving out strong light.

burr a sharp prickly covering on seeds or plants.

cater make and deliver food and give other services for a price.
ca′ ter

character 1. person in a play, book, poem or story: *Joan played the character of "Alice" in "Alice in Wonderland."* 2. the qualities that make one person, group or thing different from another.
char′ ac ter

chiffon fluffy and light; a kind of pie.
chif fon′

chops the jaws or mouth on a person or animal: *The cat licked its chops after eating.*

chowder a thick cream soup made with fish or clams, and vegetables.
chow′ der

circle a closed, round line.
cir′ cle

clatter a rattling noise.
clat′ ter

concrete cement, pebbles, sand, and water mixed together. When dry, it hardens and is used to make buildings, sidewalks, and bridges.
con′ crete′

conference a meeting: *We had a conference to discuss the problem.*
con′ fer ence

counter a long table in a store or library: *He laid his money on the counter.*
coun′ ter

croquette a small amount of fish, meat, or vegetables covered with crumbs and fried.
cro quette′

daybreak the time in the

morning when light is first seen; dawn.
day′ break′

design 1. the way colors or parts are arranged or repeated; pattern: *The design in her dress is pretty.* 2. plan or drawing used as a guide to do or make something: *This design shows how the room will look when it is finished.*
de sign′

destroy wreck; ruin.
de stroy′

dike a high wall or dam built to hold back large amounts of water, like in a sea or river.

disguise change or hide the way a person looks in order to look like someone or something else: *The actor wore sunglasses to disguise who he was.*
dis guise′

dodge move quickly to one side; move away from something in order to get away: *He had to dodge the speeding bike.*

drawbridge a bridge that can be raised and lowered. It is usually over water.
draw′ bridge′

dreadful awful; very bad; terrible: *It was a dreadful movie.*
dread′ ful

dune a small hill of sand that has been piled up by the wind.

dye 1. a substance that is used to change the color of cloth, food, hair, or other things: *I need to get some more yellow dye.* 2. color or stain: *I want to dye this skirt red.*

eager 1. very interested in something; want something very much. 2. excited.
ea′ ger

encyclopedia book or set of books that tells about all kinds of people, places, and things.
en cy′ clo pe′ di a

exhaust 1. become very tired. 2. use up.
ex haust′

exhibit show, put on display.
ex hib′ it

exist continue to be; be real; live: *Dinosaurs do not exist anymore.*
ex ist′

factory place where things are made.
fac′ tor y

ferocious look or act very mean and scary.
fe ro′ cious

fertile able to grow a large amount of plants easily; rich land. *This is a very fertile valley.*
fer′ tile

fiber hair; thread: *The coat is made from wool fiber.*
fi′ ber

flurry a short and sudden commotion or activity: *The snow flurry lasted only ten minutes.*
flur′ ry

forecast tell what may happen; predict: *The forecast is for rain on Monday.*
fore′ cast′

fret worry

fury wild, fierce anger; rage: *In his fury he knocked over the chair.*
fur′ y

gap opening; hole: *Go through the gap in the fence.*

gay having a lot of bright colors.

glass 1. material that can be seen through and that breaks easily. 2. a container which holds liquids.

glisten shine very brightly; sparkle.
glis′ ten

gloomy dark: *The basement was very gloomy.*
gloom′ y

gnaw bite or chew on until it is gone or broken: *The mouse gnawed on the cheese.*

gnome a very, very, small imaginary character, like an elf, that lives in the ground.

grace beauty of movement or manner: *She dances with so much grace.*

greedy always wanting more.
greed′ y

grieve be very sad; make very sad: *He grieved over the loss of his dog.*

guilty having done something wrong; deserving to be blamed and punished.
guilt′ y

gush rush out quickly; pour out: *The water was gushing into the pool.*

gutter ditch along the side of a road or street that carries off water.
gut′ ter

heap large pile; large amount.

herb a plant or parts of a plant used for seasoning foods, or as medicine, or perfume.

hind back; rear: *The dog stood up on its hind legs.*

hurricane bad storm with heavy rain and a very strong wind.
hur′ ri cane

hymn a song of praise.

ingredient one of many parts that make up a mixture: *One of the ingredients in the soup is carrots.*
in gre′ di ent

jolt sudden jerk, shock, or movement.

knead press, roll, and squeeze with the hands.

lather foam made from soap and water; soap bubbles.
lath′ er

least smallest; lowest in importance.

legend story about people or things that happened long ago that might be true, but cannot be proven.
leg′ end

librarian person trained to take care of a library.
li brar′ ian

long-legged having long legs.
long′ leg′ ged

243

loom frame or machine used for weaving.

lullaby song with which to sing a child to sleep.
lul′ la by

make-believe pretend.
make′ be lieve′

Martian someone or something from Mars.
Mar′ tian

meter a unit that measures length in the metric system. A meter equals a little more than 3⅓ feet: *Her dad is over two meters tall.*
me′ ter

mill a building which has machines inside to grind grain into flour or meal.

miserable extremely unhappy; very bad: *Stephanie felt miserable about losing her new ring.*
mis′ er a ble

molasses thick, sweet syrup.
mo las′ ses

monstrous very, very large.
mon′ strous

muffler 1. a scarf worn around the neck for warmth. 2. something used to reduce noise: *The muffler must be broken on that noisy car.*
muf′ fler

narrator person who tells or relates a story.
nar′ ra tor

Navajo having to do with a group of Native Americans living in New Mexico, Arizona, and Utah; a member of this group.
Nav′ a jo

neighborhood small area in a town or city where people live.
neigh′ bor hood

nervous tense, excited, or upset.
nerv′ ous

noose a loop of rope or string with a special knot that lets the loop tighten when the rope or string is pulled.

normal like most others; regular; usual.
nor′ mal

numb having no feeling; unable to move.

off-stage located or happening in the area behind or on the sides of the stage; area that cannot be seen by the audience; off the stage.
off′ stage′

one-half one of two equal parts of something.
one′ half′

outrageous shocking; bad or insulting; shameful: *They spent an outrageous amount on clothes.*
out ra′ geous

pattern design; the way shapes, colors, or lines are arranged or repeated: *The curtains had a pretty flowered pattern.*
pat′ tern

physician doctor.
phy si′ cian

pike a large freshwater fish with a long, thin body, a narrow, pointed head, and a large mouth with many sharp teeth.

pity a feeling of sorrow for the suffering or unhappiness of another.
pit′ y

planet one of the nine large bodies that revolve around the sun.
plan′ et

pluck pull off; pick: *He will pluck that flower.*

pout push out the lips to show unhappiness: *Marie is pouting because she cannot go with them.*

prop 1. an object used in a play or movie: *One of the props Little Red Riding Hood will need in this play is a red cape.* 2. hold up or hold in position by putting something under or against: *She will prop up the broken table with a chair.*

public having to do with or for all the people: *Anyone may sit in the public park.*
pub′ lic

puzzle 1. confuse or be difficult to understand: *The riddle puzzled him.* 2. problem that is done for

fun: *This jigsaw puzzle has many pieces.*
puz′ zle

rear 1. rise up on the back legs: *The horse reared when it heard the loud noise.* 2. the part that is behind or in the back.

rectangle a four-sided figure which has four right angles.
rec′ tan′ gle

reins narrow straps attached to a part of an animal's harness which help guide and control the animal: *The horse will stop if you pull on the reins.*

rejoice filled with joy; to be very glad: *The family rejoiced when they heard the good news.*
re joice′

rumble make a deep, rolling sound: *The truck rumbled down the street.*
rum′ ble

run-of-the-mill average; regular; ordinary.
run′ of the mill′

rustle make a soft, gentle, fluttering sound: *The flags rustle in the breeze.*
rus′ tle

salmon a large fish that has light pink to orange flesh.
salm′ on

satellite a man-made object that revolves around our planet in space.
sat′ el lite

scrape 1. scratch by rubbing against something rough: *Try not to scrape your leg on that rock.* 2. clean off by rubbing with something sharp: *Scrape the mud off your boots with this stick.*

scurry move quickly: *The squirrel scurried up the tree.*
scur′ ry

seize take hold of; take or grab suddenly.

sensation strong or excited feeling.
sen sa′ tion

shimmer shine with a flickering light; sparkle.
shim′ mer

short-cut a quicker way; a more direct route.
short′ cut′

shrewd clever, tricky; having a sharp mind: *That man is very shrewd.*

shriek make a loud, sharp cry or sound: *Debbie let out a shriek when she saw the burglar.*

shudder tremble from cold or fear: *I shudder every time I think about scary movies.*
shud′ der

shutter a window cover which can be opened or closed.
shut′ ter

signal warn, direct, or inform: *The officer signaled the driver to stop the car.*
sig′ nal

skin 1. cut, scrape, or damage the outer covering of the body. 2. the outer layer of the body of people and animals.

solemn 1. gloomy; serious. 2. sacred.
sol′ emn

spindle a round stick used for spinning cotton or wool into thread by hand.
spin′ dle

spot 1. see: *Where did you spot his car?* 2. a small mark or stain.

spy 1. see: *I can spy the park from here.* 2. person who secretly watches others.

strain 1. use to the extreme limit; hurt or weaken: *She strained her back lifting that box.* 2. pull with extreme force: *The tiger strained at its leash.*

strand a hair or thread: *A strand of hair fell over her eye.*

swallow a small bird that has long pointed wings and a forked tail.
swal′ low

sway move from side to side as if swinging: *As soon as the band started, people began to sway to the music.*

tattered ragged, torn.
tat′ tered

thoroughly completely.
thor′ ough ly

tile baked piece of clay or stone used to cover roofs, floors, and walls: *We have blue tile in our bathroom.*

time point when something happens: *I get lost every time I go to the store.*

toll pay for a certain service: *You have to pay a toll to cross the bridge.*

trestle a framework of crossed beams to hold up a railroad track or a bridge.
tres′ tle

triangle 1. a three-sided figure. 2. a musical instrument, made of metal and shaped like a triangle.
tri′ an′ gle

trickle flow or fall in drops in a small stream: *Water trickled down the side of the building.*
trick′ le

trough long, narrow container that holds food or water for farm animals.

typical like all others: *It was a typical day.*
typ′ i cal

weapon object used for fighting.
weap′ on

weep cry.

well 1. feel better; in good health. 2. a hole dug in the earth to get water, oil, or gas.

windmill a tall machine that uses the wind to pump water from beneath the ground.
wind′ mill′

wonderment surprise, awe, amazement.
won′ der ment

wrung squeezed or twisted together: *She wrung out a lot of water from the towel.*

yield give; give up; produce: *The garden will yield a lot of vegetables this year.*

"Lisa and the Grompet" adapted from LISA AND THE GROMPET by Patricia Coombs. Copyright © 1970. Reprinted by permission of Lothrop, Lee & Shepard (A Division of William Morrow and Co.).

"The Muffin Muncher" adapted from THE MUFFIN MUNCHER by Stephen Cosgrove (A Serendipity Book). Copyright © 1974. Reprinted by permission of Price/Stern/Sloan Publishers, Inc.

"April Rain Song" from THE DREAM KEEPER by Langston Hughes. Copyright © 1932 and renewed 1960 by Langston Hughes. Reprinted by permission of Alfred A. Knopf, Inc.

"The Hole in the Dike" adapted from THE HOLE IN THE DIKE as retold by Norma Green. Text copyright © 1974 by Norma B. Green. Reprinted by permission of Scholastic Book Services, a division of Scholastic, Inc.

"Jonathan George" by Jo Hershberger, from CHILDREN'S PLAYMATE magazine, copyright © 1973 by The Saturday Evening Post Company, Indianapolis, Indiana. Adapted by permission of the publisher.

Photo Credits

Cover photo: Hank Morgan/Rainbow; p. 14: (left) Malachuk/Taurus Photos, (right) Ernest Braun/Image Bank; p. 15: Charles Weckler/Image Bank; p. 38: (top) Russ Kinne/Photo Researchers, (bottom) Steven Langerman; p. 39: Steven Langerman; p. 40: Grant Heilman; p. 41: Steven Langerman; p. 42: (top) Russ Kinne/Photo Researchers, (bottom) Steven Langerman; p. 43: Georg Gerster/Rapho/Photo Researchers; p. 44: Michal Heron/Woodfin Camp & Associates; p. 54: The Granger Collection.

Art Credits

Bill and Judie Anderson: pp. 137–156; Jan Brett: pp. 80–89; Penny Carter: pp. 79, 122–127; Patricia Coombs: pp. 1–11; Carolyn Croll: pp. 200–210; Diane Dawson: pp. 22–31; C. S. Ewing: pp. 116–119; Hal Frenck: pp. 48–58; Tom Garcia: pp. 105, 106, 165, 166, 192–199; Ethel Gold: pp. 95–103; Meryl Henderson: pp. 157, 158, 211, 212; Francis Livingston: p. 33; Lucinda McQueen: pp. 128–136; Karen Milone: pp. 224–238; Sal Murdocca: pp. 12, 21, 32, 45, 63, 78, 90, 91, 104, 120, 121; Diane Paterson: pp. 107–115; Dale Payson: pp. 65–77; Jan Pyk: pp. 92, 93; Tony Rao: pp. 180–191; Steven Schindler: pp. 167–179; Joel Snyder: pp. 213–223; Pat Stewart: p. 13; Bill Ternay: pp. 34–37; Kyuzo Tsugami: pp. 16–20; Lynn Uhde: pp. 59–62; James Watling: p. 64; Lane Yerkes: pp. 159–164.

PHONICS CHART
Sound/Symbol Relationship Sequence

Starting Out, A

/a/aA (ant)
/n/nN (nest)
/r/rR (run)
/d/dD (dog)
/u/uU (up)
/m/mM (map)

/p/pP (pin)
/i/iI (in)
/s/sS (sun)
/o/oO (on)
/t/tT (ten)
/e/eE (egg)

/g/gG (game)
/k/cC (can)
/h/hH (hat)
/f/fF (fan)

Exploring, B

ar (art)
−er (farmer, runner)
−ed (ended, farmed, dropped)
/w/wW (win, warm, swan)
aw (saw)
ow (cow)
/l/lL, ll (let, all)

/b/bB (bed)
−le (apple)
/k/kK (kitten)
/k/ck (sack)
nk (bank)
/ā/a_e (made)
are (care)
/ē/e, ee (we, see)
/ē/ea (eat)

/ā/ai (rain)
/ī/i, i_e, ie (find, nine, pie)
ir (bird)
/ō/o, o_e (go, note)
or, ore (for, more)
/ō/oa, oe (coat, toe)
/j/jJ (jam)
/v/vV (vote)

Reaching Higher, C

sh (she)
ch, −tch (chin, catch)
th (then)
wh (what)
qu (queen)
xX (box)
yY (yes)
zZ (zip)
−ng (song)
−ing (jumping, sailing, winning, smiling)

−ed (handed, needed, stopped, waved)
−er (other, longer, baker, swimmer)
ir, ar, or, ur (girl, dollar, work, fur)
/ā/−ay (day)
/ī/−y (my)
/ē/−y, −ey, (happy, key)
/lē/−ly (safely)
soft c (cent, circus, fancy)

soft g (germ, giant, stingy)
−dge (edge)
−sion, −tion (admission, decision, motion)
short oo (book)
long oo (moon)
ow (slow)
ou (out, four, soup, your, young)
u, u_e (music, rule)
ue, ui (blue, suit)

Jumping Up, D

Formal review of sound/symbols in Texts, A,B,C
oi, oy (oil, boy)

ew, eau (few, beauty)
aw, au (saw, pause)
ph (photo)
gh (laugh)

ch (echo, machine)
silent w (write)
silent k (knit)

Rolling Along, E

silent b, l (comb, talk)
silent g, h, gh (sign, hour, right)
ea (head, great)
ear (earn, bear, heart)

/ē/ie, ei (field, ceiling)
/ā/ei, eigh, ey (vein, eight, they)
ough (rough, cough, bought, though, bough, through)
/i/y (myth)

/ī/uy, ui (buy, guide)
/i/ui (build)
/ə/ai (captain)
/e/ue (guess)
/əl/ile (missile)
silent t (listen)
silent n (autumn)

3 5 7 9 11 13 15 17 19 20 18 16 14 12 10 8 6 4